GREAT WESTERN ADVENTURE

Brian Hollingsworth

David & Charles
Newton Abbot   London   North Pomfret (VT)

British Library Cataloguing in Publication Data

Hollingsworth, J. B.
  Great Western Adventure.
  1. Great Western Railway (Great Britain)
  — History
  I. Title
  385'.0942   HE3020.G8

  ISBN 0–7153–8108–3

Photoset by
Northern Phototypesetting Company, Bolton
and printed in Great Britain
by Biddles Ltd, Guildford, Surrey
for David & Charles (Publishers) Limited
Brunel House   Newton Abbot   Devon

Published in the United States of America
by David & Charles Inc
North Pomfret   Vermont 05053   USA

Contents

Acknowledgements

The author wishes to thank the many people who helped him with this book. In particular, Graham Perry and the members of the Great Western Society who produced information and reminiscences, especially Michael Baker who chose some excellent photographs from the Society's archives. Patrick Whitehouse and John Gretton are also amongst those who gave up time to tell their stories. Special thanks are due to Margot Cooper who had the thankless task of typing out the manuscript from a spidery original.

1 Great Western Magic

The late Dr Eric Treacy, Bishop of Wakefield, that most distinguished of railway enthusiasts, was once heard to remark 'I could say anything I liked in public about religion and no one would pay the slightest attention ... but if I said the Great Western was a rotten railway I'd get 50 letters in the morning'. The occasion was the naming of LMS 4–6–0 No 5428 – a locomotive of GWR inspiration it should be added – after him. It is the passionate devotion and partisanship reflected in this remark that is the motivation of bands of dedicated people – the Great Western Society and others – to re-create just a touch of the glory that was the old GWR and which this book is all about. Not one of the other three large railway companies, which became British Railways on 1 January 1948, has inspired any comparable preservation enterprise. Neither the LMS Society nor the two LNER Societies have any known interest in this direction and the Southern Locomotive Preservation Company has only one untypical SR locomotive. A good deal of equipment belonging to these companies has been rescued but it has not been done under the banner of their names. Even so, in the bare figures of steam locomotives preserved the GWR has pre-eminence with 107 examples, the LMS with 69 (out of a fleet nearly double the size) being its nearest rival. The others (SR 52, LNER 32, BR 29) are just nowhere.

To see these 107 locomotives, one would have to visit 34 sites and one's journey would need to range as far as the outback of Western Australia. Their condition varies from stripped carcases awaiting restoration, having spent many years exposed to the damp salt-laden air of South Wales, to some of the most elegantly decorated and polished examples of the locomotive preservationist's art. At a further 21 sites one can find Great Western rolling stock, making 55 in all where GWR wheeled equipment is displayed, stored or is undergoing restoration.

Great Western tracks are used at 14 locations as tourist

railways, although this is totally eclipsed by British Rail's own operation on Great Western Railway routes, amounting to some 2,000 miles out of the old company's mileage of 3,800; many of the original structures are still carrying the modern version of the traffic for which they were designed. Although GWR trains have almost (but not quite) disappeared from BR, it is a pleasure to record that the High Speed Trains, which run on the principal main lines of the Western Region, lead the world in speed and comfort, just as those of the GWR did 50 years ago; between these times there was a long sad interval of indifference.

As well as this past pre-eminence in speed and comfort a major factor in the Great Western Railway's dominance of the preservation movement is certainly the length of its history; the GWR existed for 88 years longer than the other three, celebrating its centenary, still using its original name as the Great Western Railway Company, in August 1935. In that month it had much to be proud of; its ordinary shares were a good deal further from being in the wall-paper category (GWR Ordinary stood at 48, SR at 30, LMS at 18 and LNER at $2\frac{1}{4}$) than those of the others.

As it should be, safety was an even duller matter on the Western than any other major railway in the world. Of relations with its staff as well as with its public, it seems now to the writer (having been both) that they were pretty fair by absolute standards and, by comparative ones, fabulous. More GWR trains in proportion to their mileage were booked start-to-stop at over a mile-a-minute. And so we could go on . . . but none of such solid virtue explains the magical inspiration; other long-established, well-run, successful and beneficial institutions have gone unmourned to their graves and we have wept no tears. Why was the Great Western so special?

Well, it certainly was in 1935; imagine your author as a boy of 12, living in a house overlooking both LMS and LNER main lines, and also well acquainted with crack trains on the Southern and thus without any built-in pro-GWR bias, going to Paddington for the Cornish Riviera Limited (to visit Grandmama at Falmouth) and finding one of the Centenary trains then a few days old. Moreover, it was not, as many people have written when pondering this problem, only the crack trains which had the magic for a youngster; the sharp operation of the little Falmouth branch trains at the other end of the journey had it just the same. Having once got hold, the GWR did not let go, because although he might look out of the window back at home as the Royal Scot passed at tea time – incidentally, usually hauled by a locomotive for which a Great Western designer was responsible – he could always return to the famous and never excelled shilling 'Boys of all Ages' books, published by the GWR, once the train had passed.

An indication of the success of this excellent combination of performance and propaganda, as well as a most remarkable and prophetic sign of what was to come in preservation days, could be seen each Easter before the war at the Model Railway Club's annual exhibition in London. Stands for members' work were provided, one for each of the four great companies; the GWR was embarrassingly dominant in a very similar proportion to the figures relating to locomotive preservation today. Moreover, it was clear from the quality of the display that the Western choice had been made from an even greater number. The extraordinary thing is that the magic works both ways; we not only admire the marvellous elegance of the company's standardised locomotive fleet (locomotive cost per mile was another and little known matter in which the GWR was economically pre-eminent) but at the same time are vastly intrigued by the absurd and unnecessary variety of its coaches.

One could know the Great Western in this superficial way and easily find it outstanding, but for those lucky enough to see it at closer quarters it would be better still, as the writer found when in 1946 he became an engineering pupil at Paddington. Later experience of LMS and LNER practice and some objective thinking long afterwards has never changed his conclusion that the immunity of the Western to major accidents caused by permanent way defects, several of which occurred during the bad war and post-war period when steel and timber were rationed, was as far from a coincidence as it was on the operating side where the Automatic Warning System came 50 years before general installation elsewhere. The GWR had two major things right: first, GWR chairbolts (which went right through the sleeper up from the underside) had certain drawbacks, but at least held the rails close enough to the correct 4ft 8½in gauge long after sleepers had reached a point of ripeness where the others' coach-screws and ferrules would have given way and put something on the floor; second, A. S. Quartermaine, the Chief Engineer of the GWR in 1946 (like Brunel a century earlier he did not use the word 'Civil' in his title – only in his ways) was one whole administrative level closer to the man on the ground than his counterparts on other lines (two levels in the case of the LMS).

Not that everything was perfect or even done better than others; the practice of designing custom-made junction layouts was fine instead of wangling in standard bits until something broke. Even though one could then ring X-shop at Swindon, where they would make the special switch, crossing or whatever, and send it to you in an amazingly short time, the whole process while certainly magnificent was rather unnecessary.

The only conclusion is that while the old company did many good things, and a few bad ones, whatever it did, it did in its own remarkable way; its employees and customers, recognising this, loved it for its virtues and forgave it for its faults.

This book is an attempt to set down the immense amount that has been done to keep green the memory of the GWR, and, in addition, to pay tribute to the people who have done it. One should say that so far as this book is concerned, the Great Western Railway came to an end at midnight on that sad day, 31 December, 1947; after that, the only artifacts which count are those built to GWR designs. For example, the story of the efforts to preserve any of the independent creations of the management of BR's Western Region must be left for another chronicler. On the other hand, items that were only briefly or fortuitously in the hands of the real Great Western and have survived are included.

2 The biggest name in preservation

If one thinks about it, the biggest contribution towards preserving Great Western things comes from that unjustly despised and often vilified organisation called British Railways. Far greater, in some ways, than the modest successes of the Great Western preservers in restoring a few GW trains, is the equally exciting professional adventure of keeping alive GWR structures. Of 12,000 GWR bridges, for example, some 85 per cent are still in existence and 60 per cent of these are still being useful one way or another. Many are also very pleasing to gaze upon; one might add that the likelihood of our grandchildren's grandchildren being able to do so, too, is far greater than in the case of preserved GWR locomotives and rolling stock. Hence the pride of place given to this chapter in the book.

Perhaps your author is biased towards such things for he is proud and happy to say that a few (a very few) minor Great Western structures were conceived as pencil lines on his own drawing board. But while hundreds of junior draughtsmen have made their mark (literally) on the West of England scenery with extant artifacts, only one giant of a man bestrides Great Western civil engineering. Even today the whole system is still indelibly marked with the unmistakable stamp of Isambard Kingdom Brunel, whose personality and style combined great technical insight with excellent artistic taste.

It was a fairly young Brunel who first rode out of Bristol on 9 March 1833 to begin choosing a route for the Great Western Railway. From then until that sad occasion 26 years later when, with his health failing, he was drawn (on a trolley) across his great bridge linking England and Cornwall at Saltash, he put in several ordinary men's lifetimes of work in building the lines that came to form the GWR.

The first contract was let by the company in November 1835 soon after its Bill became law on 31 August. This was for the construction of Wharncliffe Viaduct, at Hanwell, Middlesex.

Widened now on the north side to take four standard-gauge (4ft 8½in) lines instead of two broad gauge (7ft 0¼in) tracks, this handsome structure of eight arches, when seen from the south (the best view is over what are still amazingly green fields from the A4020 Uxbridge Road just west of the Viaduct Inn), still appears just as Brunel laid it out on his drawing board all those years ago. It is also in excellent condition, having, like all Brunel's masonry structures, stood the passage of time far better than those of his successors. Certainly on the London Division in the late 1940s, the neglect of the war years was causing anxiety and expense on the 30-year old structures of the Birmingham line, rather than the 100-year old ones of the original Bristol route. Brunel himself is long gone, his body buried in Hanwell cemetery close by this No 1 artifact of the GWR. Yet first-hand evidence of his thinking and erudite design work in creating it is still with us and to be found in his General Calculation Book, now preserved at Bristol University.

Although Brunel's efforts at railway motive power (the early GWR locomotives and the atmospheric railway system in South Devon) were disasters, he would certainly have approved of the diesel High Speed Trains which roar across and under and through his bridges and tunnels all the way to Exeter and beyond. Indeed, they have finally (but only modestly, considering the time that has elapsed) eclipsed the running time from Paddington to Exeter of 4 hours 10 minutes, including stops, achieved on the opening day, 1 May 1844, with schedules (via Bristol) of 84 minutes less. This is some indication that the success of the HST in the West of England is due as much to the foresight of the civil engineer who originally designed the railway as to the mechanical engineer who designed the trains 130 years later.

Alas, taking one of the HST drawn up under Brunel's great roof at Paddington (easily recognisable today from Frith's famous picture of 1854) is not the best way to see the great man's other works, except for Paddington station itself, of course. A Brunel tour down to the West would need to employ stopping trains and road transport. Ideally, I suppose, now that the equivalent of the great man's famous *britszka* carriage – for travelling, working, eating and sleeping – is available off the shelf, and a motorhome would be the right means of making the trip.

For the first 53 miles to Didcot (a place of which there will be much more in succeeding chapters) the doubling of the original two tracks to four and much else has overlaid all but the biggest of the earlier structures. After Hanwell, the next one worth a detour is the amazing brick-built arched bridge across the River Thames between Taplow and Maidenhead. The two arches were so flat and their spans so wide (the rise was only 24ft for a span of 128ft) that the pundits of the day (and arches were well understood even in those high and far-off times) forecast collapse as soon as the centering and false-work were removed. Although, after some early and disconcerting movement, all was well, Brunel in spite of his genius seemingly listened to what others told him and left the centering up for a longer period as a precaution. In due time the centering blew down, but the bridge did not.

Apart from the road bridges, which were originally of timber, the famous Sonning cutting, just before Reading, is a piece of near-original preserved Brunel railway as well as a fabulous achievement for pick-and-shovel methods. The two additional lines were discreetly accommodated by building low retaining walls provided later at the foot of each cutting slope. Another Thames bridge, between Reading and Didcot, is of the same genre as Maidenhead, though not quite so big and not so accessible. Beyond Didcot towards Swindon and beyond, over lengths where the original double track has stayed double, the first of very many small Brunel bridges in their original state can be seen and admired. The wide space between adjacent up and down lines, a legacy of the broad gauge, is in most places apparent.

In spite of his single-minded dedication, Brunel was good company. The tale is told of his survey party spending an evening in an inn here in the Vale of the White Horse. The horse-oriented landowners had been causing them much trouble by their opposition and one of the party suggested that he would like one night to change the actual White Horse on the hill above into a locomotive. Brunel instantly took out his pocket book and worked the scheme out – how many square yards of turf to remove to expose the white chalk, how many men needed to do the whole transformation between dusk and dawn, etc. Happily, this is one piece of Brunel's work that is not there to be preserved!

Brunel did fail to foresee trains which would run all the way to Penzance in the far west of Cornwall, without needing servicing;

his railway was then laid out so that very flat gradients ruled from Paddington to Swindon. Trains would then change to smaller-wheeled locomotives for steeper gradients – inclines, the GWR always called them. All the small- and large-wheeled broad-gauge locomotives have vanished without trace, but the inclines persist in the hilly country beyond Swindon, plus the costliest and most difficult Brunel construction of them all.

Box tunnel is over 1.8 miles long and was built of ample size to accommodate broad gauge trains 15ft 6in high and 11ft wide, so BR's new trains 13ft high by 9ft wide, can be amply accommodated. Work began in 1836 and was not finished until mid-1841; the completion of the tunnel was the governing factor in the opening of the line to Bristol on 30 June 1841. The drawings for Box tunnel (and most other Great Western structures) have naturally been preserved as working documents in the drawing store of BR Western Region civil engineer.

The mystery concerning Box tunnel is that originally (as reported in the *Daily Telegraph* of 12 April, 1859) on 9 April each year, Brunel's birthday, the rising sun shines right through the tunnel, which slopes upwards towards the east on a rising gradient of 1 in 100. The actual date seems now to be a day or two different as leap years play their part in aligning dates to the earth's orbital time round the sun but it is hard to imagine that the date itself or a near miss is a coincidence. Brunel, a most erudite mathematician, would have had no difficulty in doing the calculations required, but showmanship was something he thought little of as witness a last-minute reduction in span of the big bridge at Saltash. This meant that instead of having a span of 465ft, 5ft larger than the then biggest span railway bridge in the world (Stephenson's Menai Bridge), it became 5ft less. But the decision on the gradient and line of Box tunnel was made 15 years earlier than the span at Saltash and a younger Brunel might not have been able to resist this more subtle piece of showmanship. Even so, no doubt some future civilisation on this island will speculate endlessly on such matters, just as we do on the setting out of not-too-far-off Stonehenge. For anyone wishing to do some first hand research on the problem, that motorhome would be useful, but please get permission first because BR, not wishing to be involved in the messy deaths of thoughtless people, jealously guards its property rights as, indeed, did the GWR before it.

The railway through the ancient and elegant city of Bath has much preserved of Brunel's; the lovely curved retaining walls alongside Sydney Gardens, for example, and the fine viaduct leading into the station, even if some of the original Bathstone has been patched with engineering bricks. The station itself has changed from the day when Brunel himself described the arrangements to Charles Saunders, Superintendent of the Line:

> Bath Station. I have only fenced off pens for the 2nd and 1st Class on the Up platform. On the Down platform I have not done anything yet because I could not satisfy myself as to the best mode, and it appears to me that as there are waiting rooms (at street level) below for both classes, you could manage a short time . . .

E. T. McDermott (in his superb official *History of the Great Western Railway*) dryly comments: 'Third class travellers are not provided for; doubtless they were loaded and unloaded at the adjacent goods shed, or on the platform at times when respectable people were not about.'

At Bristol Temple Meads station, there still exists the original Brunel train shed, still easily recognisable from that famous early lithograph by J. C. Bourne. After many years of rather less select use by trains of Bristol's other railway, the LMS or London Midland Region, the building is now finishing an even more undignified career as a car park; but takeover as a Brunel Museum is now imminent.

The route of the Bristol & Exeter Railway was mostly easy going but in contrast the South Devon and Cornwall sections which followed were exceptionally difficult and remarkable. From Starcross to Teignmouth lies the spectacular and famous stretch along the seashore, the preservation of which means a constant struggle against the forces of Davy Jones. It was along here that the notorious atmospheric system was tried and came to grief; one or two of the pumping station buildings survive, by chance rather than deliberately, and the odd cast-iron pipe from the famous pipeline laid between the rails can be found serving some other useful purpose.

On our journey west, the Great Western's and Brunel's greatest bridge has still to come. The Royal Albert bridge over the River Tamar at Saltash near Plymouth, has two main spans of 455ft, as well as a clear height of 100ft above the highest high water to clear the masts of naval vessels. The design, the building and the continued preservation of this enormous iron structure, carrying with only minor modification the much heavier loads of today's rail traffic, reflects the greatest credit on all concerned.

Brunel's unique combination of the principles of the arch, the suspension chain and the girder represented, in terms of weight and cost of iron-work, a 33 per cent saving on the box girders of Robert Stephenson's contemporary Britania bridge over the Menai Straits, of almost exactly the same span.

In the West there are many other lesser but still large bridges and viaducts. At Rattery, beyond Newton Abbot, came the first of Brunel's 49 famous large timber structures on the route to Falmouth (which, rather than Penzance, was the original goal of the Associated Companies – the GWR, Bristol & Exeter Railway, South Devon Railway, and the Cornwall Railway). Like the broad-gauge main-line locomotives, but not unexpectedly, none of these spidery but practical creations has been preserved and all that can now be seen of them are (at many of the locations) the masonry piers which survive. Of course, the arched viaducts which, between 1870 and 1934, replaced most of them – a few were replaced by steel structures and others by embankments or by-passes – are as much Great Western as anything that went before, even if less famous and distinctive. Perhaps they could stand in this account for the thousands of lesser viaducts, bridges, tunnels and buildings as well as stations built by the old railway and still preserved by the new one, but not mentioned in this brief account of what might be called 'useful' preservation of the GWR's more solid and lasting artifacts.

3 Early days of the Great Western Society

In 1955 British Rail announced the forthcoming end of steam, and five years later full-size railway preservation was on the move, having graduated from a purely narrow-gauge activity to the opening of the standard-gauge Bluebell Railway in Sussex in 1960. Early in 1961 the Consultative Panel on railway historical relics reported with a final list of a further 30 locomotives to be earmarked for preservation, making, together with those already set aside, a total of 71 on the official list. Of these, the Great Western rated the absurdly small share of eight as follows:

2–2–2   *North Star* (replica)
4–4–0   *City of Truro*
4–6–0   *Lode Star*
2–8–0   28XX class
0–6–0   Dean Goods
4–6–0   *Caerphilly Castle*
4–6–0   *King George V*
0–6–0 PT   94XX class

One of the particularly glaring omissions from this meagre list was a GWR branch line passenger tank locomotive, which brings us to the Founding Fathers of the Great Western Society. From what has been written in the first chapter one could imagine they were some of the Old Guard, marinated in GWR lore, who wanted to keep just a little taste of the old days to remind them of what they had loved and admired in their prime. In fact, one could not have been more wrong because, on the contrary, they were the schoolboy train spotters of Southall, who were not even a twinkle in their parents' eyes when the old line gave up a lot of its most characteristic ways on the outbreak of war in 1939.

The first positive public step was taken in the summer of 1961, when Jon Barlow on their behalf wrote a letter to the Railway Magazine, published in the August issue:

Proposed Preservation of GWR Tank

Sir,

I am thinking of launching a campaign to purchase a "14XX" (former "48XX") class 0–4–2 tank locomotive from British Railways with the purpose of preserving it in running order. The cost is £1,130 plus extras such as having "48XX" plates cast and repainting it in Great Western livery. If sufficient support is obtained, perhaps a pull-and-push coach also might be preserved. I appeal to all those who could support this suggestion to get in touch with me at 14 Heldman Close, Hounslow, Middlesex.

(signed) J. L. Barlow

The lads, returning from a gricing excursion to Scotland, were surprised and delighted to find a pile of replies and actual folding money to the tune of £25 10s 6d, a princely sum in those days. They decided on the formation of a society to be known as the '48XX Preservation Society' and pressed on with finding members and raising funds.

By the time of the inaugural meeting, they had decided to change the name and on 4 May 1962, at Southall Community Centre, the Great Western Preservation Society was launched; 90 people attended and Angus Davies was in the chair. Graham Perry acted as treasurer. Money came in steadily and by the time of the third Annual General Meeting on 1 February 1964 – held this time at St James' Hall, Paddington – the committee was able to announce that the Society's (which had now dropped the word 'Preservation' from its title) 0–4–2T No 1466 was shortly to be delivered. The price, which had amazingly fallen over the intervening $2\frac{1}{2}$ years, was £750 including delivery.

On 15 March, No 1466 was delivered under her own steam from Taunton to Staverton Contractors' Sidings at Totnes, Devon and the Great Western Society was in business. The reader may ask, why so far down the line? The reason lies in the problem faced by everyone who buys a train set, large or small, that of finding a place to play with it. Totnes was promising because a group of substance known as the Dart Valley Railway Co, were planning to re-open the branch line from there to Buckfastleigh and Ashburton and run it as a live working museum of Great Westernry. This enterprise is described in chapters seven and eight.

The Society had, in fact, been interested in an earlier attempt to preserve a Devon branch, that to Moretonhampstead, by the South Devon Railway Society. In the event sufficient funds were not forthcoming and in 1962 the SDR Society was absorbed by the Great Western Society, the events of 1876 repeating themselves.

Even this was not the first because a certain T. W. E. Roche had got a long way towards saving yet another branch in the district, that serving Kingsbridge. While he was actually negotiating with BR's regional general manager, the stores superintendent sent the scrap men in. So Tom Roche turned in 1963 to the Great Western Society. Here was no schoolboy gricer but a GWR lover dating from between the wars and, moreover, a distinguished man holding down one of the hottest jobs the country has to offer, that of chief immigration officer at London Airport.

Roche (even his name was a GWR station) became secretary and later chairman of the Reading group of the society. His status and personality were very advantageous in obtaining facilities to begin a series of open days in the London Area, which demonstrated the potentialities of independent existence for the Society, of which more anon. Alas he died in 1972 at the absurdly early age of 50.

No 1466 was joined at Totnes during the 1964 summer by the Society's first coach, Dreadnought corridor third No 3299, the result of a noble effort by bus-driver David Rouse, an indefatigable fund-raiser for GWR artifacts. In the autumn came a shunting locomotive from Plymouth Docks, 0–6–0 saddle tank 1363. It arrived in time to be in steam (literally so, since the dome joint gasket was blowing) together with 1466, at the first ever open day to be held by the Society on 17 October; 550 people attended.

Auto-coach 231, purchased by the Society in accord with their original letter of intent to run with 1466, was also sent to Totnes and early in 1965 a group of members led by Mr and Mrs Weary acquired 1369, a more modern pannier tank version of 1363.

Also in spring 1965 came the first printed and properly illustrated number of the Society's journal *Great Western Echo*. Frank Dumbleton — another of the Southall originals, then secretary of the Society and from 1967 to 1978 editor of the *Echo* — wrote an amusing account in it of a trip to Totnes on the dual occasion of the arrival of 1369 in steam from Bodmin and the inaugural meeting of the South-Western group.

The tide in the affairs of Western preservation was certainly at the flood, and our young Society now went ahead to repair the most extraordinary and inexplicable omission on the part of individually fairly well-informed and balanced people who drew up the 'official' list referred to earlier. No GWR two-cylinder 4–6–0 was down for preservation, in spite of the landmark of locomotive design they represented; as innovations they were in the class of the contemporary battleship HMS *Dreadnought* which made everything else obsolete. This time it was not 30 tons of locomotive but 110 tons and thousands not hundreds of pounds. With some trepidation a new fund was launched but this time it was not hundreds a year but thousands a month and in a few short weeks (actually on 15 January 1966) ownership of No 6998 *Burton Agnes Hall* brought the GWS into the Big Steam League. On 2 April 1966 No 6998 travelled down to Totnes.

In this way matters went on very pleasantly; indeed, the period at Totnes was a delightful interlude. Locomotives were steamed and run on the sidings there without formality by groups rushing down overnight from Middlesex and in general, fun and games were had that, although nothing untoward ever happened, make the hair of the now regulation-conscious Society officials stand on end.

Serious matters intervened, however, at Easter 1966, with a question of future involvement with the Dart Valley Railway, which had to be put to members in the form of a ballot. This was the moment when the Society really found itself, and the management committee decided on independence with indeterminate prospects rather than the soft option of being a supporters club of the Dart Valley Railway Company. Until then Society policy had been to work for the joint establishment of the live GWR museum on the Totnes to Ashburton branch. However, the DVR management's terms involved (for, from their point of view, very good reasons) a complete abdication of sovereignty over the Society's precious acquisitions in exchange for shares which might or might not in due time like railway shares other than those of the GWR fall into the wallpaper category. The result of the ballot was:

For integration	Against integration
408	31

Democracy opted soft but with the true Nelson touch, treasurer Graham Perry 'clapped his glass to his sightless eye' with the comment:

The Management Committee would like to remind all members that this was a vote recording how members felt on the document put forward. This being so, the Management Committee reserves the right to act otherwise in extenuating circumstances.

Integration did not take place and in due course Graham became and remains Chairman.

All parties benefited; as is to be described in the next chapter, the Society eventually obtained a lease of the depot at Didcot and, at the same time, the DVR Co formed its own supporters club which helped it to buy and run the railway. One slight regret is the fate of pannier tank No 1369, which was purchased in 1965 by a group of GWS members, who in fact opted for it to stay in Devon, where, being too small for commercial traffic purposes, it has not been cherished as it would have been as an ideal open day locomotive at Didcot.

Speaking of open days, 15 September 1966 was a milestone in the Society's history, when for the first time its own locomotives were exhibited in the London area at Taplow station near Maidenhead. An amazing 7,000 people attended, to some extent swamping the organisation, to see 4079 *Pendennis Castle*, 7808 *Cookham Manor* (which arrived on a railtour from Birmingham) and 2-6-2T No 6106 as well as ride in super-saloons 9112, 9113 and 9118. It was this sort of attendance figure that demonstrated the potentiality of a working museum in the Home Counties and the rightness of the Management Committee's decision to remain independent and seek a suitable site within reach of London. Moreover, by then the Western Region was steamless for everyday operation, and the only regular steam was on the Southern's Bournemouth line which had only a few months more to run.

The first number of *Great Western Echo* in which the cover looks anything like those of the present day, was No 15, the summer issue 1965. It is notable for two appeals for funds, one for 7029 *Clun Castle* and the other for 0-6-0 No 3205. In spite of this, both locomotives although now in good hands, were lost to the Society. The latter, together with Dukedog 4-4-0 No 9017, which had already been preserved independently, had gone, *faut de mieux*, to the Bluebell Railway, and represent gaps in the Society's collection which are never likely to be filled. Shortly afterwards, as has been related, the young GWS was all but swallowed up by the Dart Valley Railway. All these failures and that (for them) near catastrophe stemmed from one thing, the lack of a patch of their own.

19

In considering any high-handedness involved in applying the Nelson touch over the Dart Valley ballot matter, it must be said that those on the quarter-deck knew something the ordinary members did not, which was that a reasonable chance existed, if the greatest care and restraint was shown, of obtaining the use of the ex-GWR motive power depot at Didcot. It was a modern depot, having been opened in 1933, including a lifting shop, plenty (or what then seemed to be plenty) of under-cover shed roads, coaling stage, messrooms, washrooms, offices and above all had an excellent local service to all stations on the London line, as well as direct trains to many other places in England and Wales.

With the closure of the Didcot, Newbury & Southampton line and neighbouring Moreton yard, together with main line dieselisation, the depot's importance had declined to a point where closure seemed inevitable. Also, bounded as it was on both sides by running lines, and without road access, it was almost valueless as an industrial site and so a possible haven for impecunious railway preservationists.

But there were problems; in the eyes of Chairman Raymond and Vice-chairman Shirley of British Railways, preservation was a naughty word and Great Western a pair of even naughtier ones. Gerard Fiennes had been put in at Paddington to complete its de-Westernisation (you can read about it in his amusing book *I Tried To Run a Railway*) but he appears to have suffered a certain Westernisation himself in the process. Again, several of the top brass of the Society had not long left school and, in the early stages of their careers found it difficult to take time off in office hours to negotiate with senior railway officials who kept identical ones. However, the hour produced, not the one man but the several, both inside and outside BR, who could, between them, carry the day.

4 Didcot develops

To begin the story of Didcot one must again go back to Great Western Echo No 15, wherein is described a high-speed tour from London to Plymouth and back, organised by Trevor Bailey of the Ian Allan Group. This was run to commemorate the 60th anniversary of the famous (and so nearly infamous) run of 4–4–0 *City of Truro* on 9 May, 1904; among the many risks taken that day was the high speed reached when going hell-for-leather down the sinuous alignment of Wellington Bank. The claimed world record speed (at that time) of 102.6mph has been disputed ever since by non-GWR writers and enthusiasts.

On the commemoration special, No 4079 *Pendennis Castle* was herself descending the better aligned Pewsey Bank at 96mph with speed still rising, when some of the firebars melted and she dropped her fire, becoming a casualty – and hence condemned – after removal from the train at Westbury. Not much was wrong beyond a hot axlebox and Chief Locomotive Inspector Jack Hancock, whose ewe lamb she was, oiled the wheels (figuratively as well as literally) in support of a bid by an ex-railwayman called Michael Higson to buy the engine, after repairs and repainting had been done at Swindon. A number of enthusiast trips were run under his ownership; during this period No 4079 was stationed and serviced at Southall where some residual steam operation remained.

On one of these outings, a young man, the Honourable John Gretton, was unwise enough to ask Inspector Hancock's advice on buying a locomotive – something fairly humble and simple for a young beginner, such as a Manor class perhaps. 'What you want Mr Gretton', said Hancock, 'is the finest locomotive in the world, the one up ahead.' John was told that if he made up his mind forthwith he could have her, as Michael Higson wanted to sell. The deal was done the next day in a Reading café; Bill McAlpine came in as a partner.

The storm broke for John a day or two later with a telephone call from another angry buyer whose cheque in payment for No 4079 had been sent back to him. It was still blowing a little while later when the new young locomotive owner was summoned to the boardroom at Paddington, only to be told by a distinguished gathering of railwaymen that they wanted his locomotive off their property.

In the chair was the divisional manager, by name David Pattisson, who was in the end the man who unlocked the Didcot door. Two things changed his mind about Mr Pendennis Castle; first, his ability to steam and service the locomotive, as demonstrated when No 4079 attended that open day at Taplow on 18 September, 1965. Second, of course, was the fact that his partner was a man whose position in the world of engineering was such that he might well normally deal with BR at chairman level. In fact, John Gretton had considerable experience with steam on the $10\frac{1}{4}$in gauge public miniature railway in the grounds of his family's stately home at Stapleford Park in Leicestershire, so his success was that much easier to explain.

In his dealings with the Pendennis Castle partnership, Pattisson had a particular problem. He was, of course, a GWR man born and bred, and accordingly had a natural sympathy for preserving one of the old line's most famous locomotives; but at that time railwaymen who indicated any sort of enthusiasm for the past were liable to be placed themselves in the past, particularly as regards any future promotion. Indeed, the Marylebone Road Kremlin had a habit of sending any such person to one of BR's many equivalents of Siberia. But David believed that this startling new concept of a depot-museum for vintage trains was a right one and to some extent put his own future at risk in order to achieve it.

Anyway, the upshot was that one day John Gretton was told that there was a small steel-built repair and lifting shop inside the depot at a place called Didcot, just down the line. In fact, when he got there the scrap men had just begun cutting up the shafting and machinery inside. Luckily the structure itself, as well as the crane which gave the building its name was still intact and there was just time to offer the scrap men's employer enough money to stay his hand.

Early in 1967 *Pendennis Castle* was worked from Southall to Didcot and placed in the lifting shop; the depot thus began its new role as a home for working museum pieces. Even so, negotiations over Didcot had to proceed with extreme care; it was a help that the Divisional Manager was dealing with two people who bore well-known names and one who was a big BR customer and contractor. Among the difficulties were the fact that there were legal problems in selling or even leasing a site that had no road access and, as well, might even be needed for traffic purposes. Even so, as BR's requirements in the depot shrunk to a single shed road, the Great Western Society's rolling stock was moved in under licence. The material from the London area, hauled by 2–6–2T No 6106, entered the depot on 4 November, 1967, while 4–6–0 *Burton Agnes Hall* and 0–4–2T 1466 plus the rolling stock came up from Devon on 18 December.

A temporary ban on special steam trains imposed by BR during that winter was lifted in time for the Society to be asked to put on a special public train service over the nearby $2\frac{3}{4}$-mile branch from Cholsey & Moulsford to Wallingford, using 0–4–2T No 1466 and trailer No 231 running as an auto-train. The day was Easter Monday, 15 April, 1968. It is very sad to relate that this excellent little operation – a success in every way – is no longer repeated. The nearest was a similar one-off operation on the Marlow branch to mark the centenary of the celebrated 'Marlow Donkey' in 1973.

About this time a sister organisation to the Great Western Society was formed; there was a feeling among those who had put down substantial sums for the purchase of rolling stock, that control of this equipment should not be vested in the Society members at large. Accordingly Great Western Preservations Limited came into being; the first Annual General Meeting was held on 13 July, 1968.

In the Spring of 1969 British Railways finally vacated the depot, leaving the way open for 10 May, 1969, a date which made history by being the first open steaming day at Didcot, with about 1,000 attending; the first fully public occasion of this kind came in the autumn, on 20 September, with 4,500 visitors. A further 'first', concerned with the profitable activities of the Society and also connected with history, occurred in June 1971 when No 1466 went down to South Wales. Rather dubiously disguised as an armoured locomotive of the South African war period, she starred in the film *The Young Winston*, which was shot on the lonely and then disused Neath & Brecon Line.

The open day in September 1971 was notable for an absolutely resplendent *Pendennis Castle* on display in steam.

This was her first public occasion since 1967 and, alas, her last, for some feeling had now arisen between the two groups of preservers in the depot. It did not seem right to the Society that the only boiler-lifting crane should not be available to them, simply because the line beneath it was used for stabling someone else's locomotive. On the other hand the owners of *Pendennis Castle* (with reason, as it turned out) felt that once they left their shed they would never get back.

The Society's hand was strengthened at this time by the departure of the Divisional Manager for higher things; they were able to obtain an agreement with Pattisson's successor, giving them exclusive rights to deal with BR over all matters concerned with Didcot. After all, they owned the majority of the equipment on site and naturally BR did not want the trouble and hassle of having separate arrangements with more than one owner in the same depot.

John Gretton was thus presented with an ultimatum – assign *Pendennis Castle* to the Society if you want to stay at Didcot. For once the Society's Nelsonian tactics did not succeed; deep down inside the apparently vague and gentle John was an iron resolve to do his own thing for steam. So, after an attempt at bluff (by putting physical obstacles in the way of her departure) *Pendennis Castle* left Didcot on 23 June 1972 for pastures new. Her subsequent and (in some ways) rather unhappy history can be traced in later chapters. It was to be nine years before the GWS had an express locomotive of its own in steam. Even so, on this date the Society found itself not only with its own depot but also in total control of everything in it, so becoming master of its own fate. Indeed, since then the story of Didcot is an account of steady progress so unchanging as to be almost boring. All the ingredients of success were there; wise and firm management, enough money coming in for essentials but not too much to encourage extravagance and waste, new rolling stock and projects to sustain interest. The climax occurred on 1 October, 1972 when, after British Railways had relented over its ban on steam locomotives, the Society worked a rail tour from Didcot to Tyseley and back with its own *Burton Agnes Hall*, newly overhauled by a group of members in the depot.

At this point the historian and the working member diverge in their views. To the former the step from the Didcot of 1972 to the Didcot of 1982 is a single natural and inevitable one, whereas the latter feels it is an insult to pass over in this way the endless hours of tedious back-breaking work interspersed with heart-breaking disappointments which are the essence of railway preservation. Not that the endurance of such trials and tribulations entitles anyone to complain that others do not join them in their way of self-fulfilment – unless those others set out to criticise – but there is certainly entitlement to some recognition of the work done. Even so, may this author express here his deepest admiration and gratitude for all the efforts made, the skills demonstrated and the results obtained.

The agreement with BR provided for fencing the site and, apart from the provision of a cafe building and the laying of a demonstration running line, at first only makeshift improvements to the accommodation could be done. Resources, both human and financial, were concentrated on acquiring material and restoring the wheeled equipment; the stupendous efforts made culminated in the Didcot working members, under the leadership of Peter Tenzing Chatman, being the first to scale the Mount Everest of preservation by running their own beautifully restored vintage coaches as a complete train, the GREAT WESTERN SOCIETY LIMITED, out on the main line from Didcot to Stratford-on-Avon. This double-headed run took place on Saturday, 19 October, 1974, and was several times over-subscribed. Many members attended this and subsequent trips in period uniform or costume. Over the next five years the vintage train steadily increased in length and its operation in scope. Even though the Didcot to Hereford line as an alternative was deleted from the list of approved routes for steam in 1977, the GWS Ltd was able to range profitably far and wide under BR diesel power – on one occasion even electric power over the Woodhead line.

Also in 1974, the Didcot operations attracted the attention of the Department of the Environment's Railway Inspectorate. The first result of this was very nearly the cancellation of the Autumn Open Day that year; the second was the erection of a proper fence to keep apparently suicidal children (and parents) away from the demonstration line. Also recommended was a proper platform for loading passengers instead of piled-up sleepers. In addition, the growing burden of administration meant dividing the depot manager's responsibilities (Peter Chatman wanted to stand down anyway) between a technical manager and a development manager.

In 1975 the Didcot Plan was announced to members. This was

an ambitious idea to turn the Didcot depot area into a Great Western showground, such a project being made possible by BR's willingness to transfer a further area inside its triangle to the Society. In April 1976, outline planning consent was obtained for a big carriage shed complete with traverser, a museum and sales building, a second running line complete with signalbox and station and, finally, a turntable. There certainly seemed to be a long haul ahead but, in the event, all the principal items were completed well ahead of target. The reason was that the good fairy Job Creation Scheme came along, waved her magic wand and lo and behold, full-time staff were on site to tackle the basics of the new work in double quick time. This left the volunteers free to attend to such details as erecting and equipping with full interlocking a typical GWR signalbox, whose structure came from Radstock, Somerset. The new No 2 demonstration line has a station at both ends; at the south end one of the famous corrugated-iron 'pagodas' shelters passengers (it came from Stockcross & Bangor Halt on the Lambourn branch), while they pay their fares at a ticket office from Welford Park on the same Lambourn Valley line.

At the north end is an historic structure, the re-erected Didcot transfer shed, built originally to transfer goods from broad-gauge to standard-gauge wagons. By a happy coincidence, some original broad-gauge track material was discovered in 1978 at a private siding site near Burlescombe, Somerset, and this has been relaid on the broad-gauge side of the shed in mixed-gauge form. So all is ready for 7ft $0\frac{1}{4}$in gauge trains at Didcot – except the trains! Talking of mixed gauge, a $3\frac{1}{2}$in/5in mixed gauge raised track is provided for live steam models, enabling steam passenger-hauling to be done but consuming ounces rather than tons of coal.

Finally, yet another 'first' and 'only' for the GWS is the operation of a travelling post office at Didcot, exchanging mail-bags at lineside apparatus alongside the No 1 demonstration line. Incidentally, the mail is real, consisting of special mail-exchange postal covers, thereby paying for the maintenance and restoration of the TPO van and its equipment. This perhaps gives a hint as to why the Great Western Society has a healthy bank balance, an income (in 1979) of some £70,000 excluding grants and an optimistic view of the future.

5 The Didcot locomotive collection

It is always a pleasant thing to pick up one's pen to write on the subject of Great Western locomotives because one cannot escape the thought that although far from perfect, they were one of mankind's greatest achievements. That harsh critic of locomotive practice in general, the late Professor Tuplin, concluded his delightful book *Great Western Steam* (George Allen & Unwin, 1958) with the words:

> Commonsense compromise between theoretical ideals and practical possibilities had produced at Swindon a unique family of standard engines unsurpassed anywhere in fitness for purpose. Shall we ever see again such distinction on the rails? We fear; we doubt; we can scarcely hope.

So much the more, therefore, does anyone with the temerity to offer a collection of such noble material render themselves open to criticism. Of the Great Western Society's examples the best compliment that can be paid is to say that it (almost) has the appropriate locomotive for every GWR haulage task from running the Cornish Riviera Limited to shunting on the docks. Taking as a counsel of perfection the 27 classes included in the last (and 29th!) edition of the famous *GWR Engine Book*, the Society has eleven of them. As we shall see, six further classes are covered elsewhere, but one has to visit four sites to find them.

Of the remaining nine classes in the book, six might be said to have been covered by the preservation of near relations, leaving only three significant gaps in the whole tour-de-force that was twentieth-century GWR locomotive engineering – a most remarkable and satisfactory achievement, to which the Didcot collection has contributed more than any other.

Equally remarkable but wholly unsatisfactory, however, is the absence, complete at Didcot and with only one honourable exception elsewhere, of any of the principal nineteenth-century GWR classes. From the whole broad gauge fleet, only one little tea kettle remains, Stephenson's original *North Star* being a

27

mere replica. It is one black mark against God's Wonderful Railway that the famous 4–2–2 *Lord of the Isles*, set aside for preservation in 1871 and afterwards exhibited in Paris and elsewhere, was cut up in 1906 on the grounds that there was no room at Swindon.

Having reviewed the quality of the GWS locomotive collection as an entity, it now remains to describe its individual components, starting with express locomotives and ending with shunting tank engines.

The Castle class was the mainstay of the Great Western express passenger services from 1923 onwards; 183 were turned out between then and 1950. They were outstanding among British express locomotives, working such varied assignments as, on the one hand the Cheltenham Flyer, the world's fastest train, and on the other the Cornish Riviera Limited in the days when it loaded almost limitlessly up to 15 70ft coaches on leaving Paddington. The figure of 2.83 lb of coal burnt per drawbar-horsepower-hour achieved by *Caldicot Castle* on test in 1924 has never been bettered in Britain. Exchange running on the LNER between Kings Cross and Leeds in 1925 and on the LMS between Crewe and Carlisle in 1926 led to major improvements in locomotive design on both these railways. The Castle class is also the only modern steam locomotive to have been honoured by appearance on a British postage stamp; this was *Caerphilly Castle* in 1975, to celebrate 150 years of steam public railways.

Of the two Didcot Castles, No 5029 *Nunney Castle* will no doubt one day be in a condition to handle a 15-coach Limited or an 81mph start-to-stop Flyer, but it is not quite the case yet. No 5029, one of the third batch completed in 1934, only came to Didcot in 1975 as a carcase fresh from 12 years in the scrapyard at Barry. No 5051 from the same source came in 1972 and was put back into service in 1980. She was built in 1936, the change of name from *Drysllwyn Castle* to *Earl Bathurst* taking place in 1937. Apparently, C. B. Collett, Chief Mechanical Engineer at the time, suffered from certain titled gentlemen on the GWR Board who were given to interfering (as he would put it) in locomotive matters. Like President Kennedy, who said 'don't get mad, get even', he expressed his feelings by naming a group of new but very small and old-fashioned locomotives after noble Earls. He drew blood in the form of protests and the nameplates were then politely transferred to the fifth and then most recent batch of Castles, 5043 to 5062. But the point was made to the end because the nameplates did not quite fit, being made to suit the splashers belonging to wheels of a smaller diameter.

The completion of the restoration of *Drysllwyn Castle/Earl Bathurst* was crowned on 4 April 1980, by a naming ceremony at Didcot. Earl Bathurst himself named one side after himself, after which the new turntable was swung and Mrs John Mynors, widow of the man who had put up the money to buy 5051, named the other. No 5051 was finished just in time to be able to perform the last runs of the now legendary vintage train. Later she showed off her brassy green beauty in the Rocket 150 Cavalcade in May, 1980. Incidentally the name *Drysllwyn Castle* was used four times, the last time for No 7018.

A drawback to the four-cylinder Castle class is the complication of having two additional complete sets of works between the frames. It has been said that the person who laid the arrangement out on paper must have been pretty certain that he personally was going to have little to do with looking after it in service. But the Great Western possessed what was almost an alternative main line fleet of two-cylinder 4–6–0 locomotives. Indeed, when what became known as the Saint class began to emerge from Swindon, at the beginning of the century, it was a landmark of landmarks in locomotive design, leading eventually to a fleet of nearly 500 4–6–0 of almost identical construction.

In 1925 the 6ft 8½in wheels of *Saint Martin* were replaced with ones of 6ft 0in diameter and thus was produced the prototype of the most numerous sub-group of the 500. The fashion for such romantic names as Saints, Ladies, Knights and Princes had passed, so all 329 of the Hall class were named after these sometimes-not-too-stately homes of England, commencing with those in GWR country and later perforce finding names from alien lands.

Two Halls are operational at Didcot, No 5900 *Hinderton Hall* from the second 1931 batch and 6998 *Burton Agnes Hall* built in 1949 and one of the last 80 with plate instead of bar frames at the front end. No 5900 was rescued from Barry in 1971, while 6998 as recorded earlier was purchased out of BR service in 1966. Both locomotives have had major overhauls at Didcot and the two performed in tandem on the Great Western Society's vintage special train in 1976. The real Hinderton Hall is near Kidderminster but Burton Agnes is far away in the East Riding of Yorkshire.

A third Hall, No 4942 *Maindy Hall* of 1929, from the first

large order for 80, awaits reverse conversion, gaining 6ft 8½in wheels in place of the 6ft 0in set and a plain cab for the windowed variety to recreate a Saint class, and using, one presumes, the vacant number 2999. The choice of name will no doubt cause controversy, but careful perusal of chapter 4 would suggest a resurrection of *Saint David*.

In 1938, to provide a modern 4–6–0 capable of running on certain secondary main lines, in particular the Cambrian routes, with weight restrictions that prohibited the Hall class, a miniaturised version was built which took the form of the 20 locomotives of the Manor class, later increased to 30. No 7808 *Cookham Manor* was bought by a member of the GWS in 1965 and has been completely restored at Didcot.

Harold Holcroft, in his book *Locomotive Adventure*, describes how, while working at Swindon in 1910, he took the opportunity of making a study tour of North America and while there took note of the use of the 2–6–0 type for mixed and general duties. On return, he suggested to Churchward that a 2–6–0 with 5ft 8in wheels would have a wide application. He was promptly given the job of producing the design which was very successful, running eventually to 323 examples. The Society's No 5322 was one of a batch built in 1917 and sent to France immediately on completion; the main task over there was the haulage of 1000-ton supply trains from Calais to 2nd Army railheads around Hazebrouck. No 5322 set the fashion for rescues from Messrs Woodham's yard at Barry, needing a special dispensation from BR for its re-sale, grudgingly given in this first instance solely on the grounds of the locomotive's historic importance, but in fact opening the door to an avalanche of hulks from this source. Nos 5322, 5051, 5900, 6998 and 7808, all currently in working order, make a strong team to show how the GWR handled all but the very top main-line trains both passenger and fast goods.

The remaining items of Great Western passenger power in the collection are the tank locomotives for short distance trains; the large, medium and small are covered. First is the standard suburban type 2–6–2T, introduced by Churchward in 1903 and being built to a total of 250 over 40 years later; of these Didcot has No 6106, built in 1931, bought out of service in 1966, and now in fully restored condition. The carcase of No 4144 (built 1946) which came from Woodhams of Barry in 1974, is in reserve.

Next in descending order of size is 45XX class 2–6–2T No

5572 of 1927, kept for several years appropriately at Taunton after rescue from Barry in 1970. The operation of West Country branches which abounded in sharp gradients, sharp curves as well as frequent and awkwardly placed stops were revolutionised by these locomotives. In these conditions their surefootedness was a byword; a major factor was the springing, equalised between the driving wheels and the pony trucks, a system standard in the USA and commonplace on the Continent but otherwise almost unknown in Britain. E. S. Cox, BR's Chief Officer (Design), says in his book *Locomotive Panorama* (Ian Allan 1965) that the absence of this feature at the rear end was a major handicap at starting in the BR Britannia 4–6–2s. He understandably does not add that his team would have done better to have taken note of what the GWR was doing 40 years before.

Finally, on the passenger side we come to the Society's first love, the delightful 0–4–2T No 1466, built as 4866 in, it might surprise the uninitiated to learn, not 1886 but 1936. It was not for the GWR to work its minor branches with discarded relics, nor to have any bashfulness about the sensible but not very fashionable course of repeating, with modernised details, a Victorian design. No 1466 and her sisters did excellent work on the auto-trains for which they were designed, speeds well up in the seventies often having been recorded.

The kings of freight on the GWR were the 167 28XX class 2–8–0s of 1903 onwards, and a recent acquisition from Barry for future restoration is No 3822 of 1940, one of the wartime batch ordered after a gap in construction of 30 years. Many parts, including the No 1 boiler, are standard with the Hall class 4–6–0. No 3822 is the only freight tender locomotive in the collection; the absence of lighter freight engines is perhaps the only chink in the contention stated earlier that the Society could provide appropriate power for any GWR train.

There was also a 2–8–0 tank locomotive design, the 42XX class built for short distance coal haulage. During the slump of the 1930s more were on hand than needed; in 1934–9 54 were renumbered, given larger coal bunkers and an extra pair of carrying wheels for main-line work. One of these rebuilds, No 7202, came to Didcot from Barry in 1975. The class was the only 2–8–2T used in Great Britain, as indeed the 42XX was the only 2–8–0T.

In 1923 the independent railways of the South Wales coal

valleys came into the GWR family and brought with them an immense but heterogenous fleet of 425 0–6–2 tank locomotives (from the Taff Vale alone came 207 out of a total locomotive stock of only 274). Many could be rebuilt to bring them into line with GW practice, but to replace the others 200 0–6–2Ts were constructed in 1927–28, mainly by outside contractors, using the No 6 boiler and other parts from the Swindon 'Meccano' set. This hard-working class was used not only on the pit-to-port coal traffic for which they were intended, but also on the smartly-timed passenger trains up and down the Valleys. No 6697, originally bought out of BR service by the Bristol Group of the Society, originated (unusually) not from Swindon but from Armstrong-Whitworth of Tyneside in 1928; exceptionally this actual engine was not one allocated to South Wales.

We come now to the numerically greatest and at the same time one of the humblest of Great Western locomotives, the 57XX class standard pannier tanks of which 863 (in a contestable photo-finish, also the most numerous class ever to run in Britain) were constructed between 1927 and 1948. They were largely copied from a much earlier design. So many were built that they torpedoed the neat but original system whereby locomotives of the same class shared the *second* digit of a four-figure number, and the newer of the Didcot examples Nos 3738 and 3650 (of 1937 and 1939 respectively) had to be put in an overflow series. The pannier tank feature made both boiler and motion more accessible than more conventional side or saddle tanks and it is odd that such a sensible arrangement was not copied by other designers. Most of their duties were of such humble kinds as shunting, trip freights etc, but it must be added that the high and mighty Cornish Riviera Limited started its movements on most mornings behind one of them, and, indeed, a pannier tank would be the only locomotive the average passenger from Paddington would see attached to it. No 3650 came from the National Coal Board in 1970 and 3738 from Barry in 1972 and they represent a very essential item for any GW or, in fact, National locomotive collection. Their omission from the 1960 official list of worthy preservations is yet another of its inexplicabilities; but they say a camel is a horse designed by a committee or, in this case, a panel.

The last true Great Western locomotive belonging to the Society is one which can really go where others cannot, even round curves of two chain (40 metres) radius and on lines too weak for more than a 10-ton axleload. Saddle tanks 1361–1365

Above: Great Western magic: No 7808 *Cookham Manor* and No 5900 *Hinderton Hall* at Henley-in-Arden on 15 October 1978 with the Great Western Society Limited vintage train. *Michael Baker*

Below: Paddington station – apart from the trains – more or less as Brunel designed it. Note the Great Western Society's vintage train in the foreground and modern trains to the left and in the background. *Courtesy Great Western Society*

Above: A rare photograph of No 4079 *Pendennis Castle* taken on 1 December 1973 during its brief sojourn at Market Overton, Rutland. *David M. Scudamore*

Below: Great Western Society; 0-4-2T No 1466, the Society's first acquisition passes Cholsey parish church on 13 April 1968, working a special Wallingford branch service. *J. R. P. Hunt*

were built in 1910 mainly for shunting on the docks at Plymouth, from where 1363 was bought out of service in 1965. Harold Holcroft describes in his reminiscences how a roll of drawings for an old Cornwall Minerals Railway tank locomotive was dumped on his drawing board one day with instructions for him to get out a modernised version. As one of the world's leading experts on valve gear, one can imagine his pleasure in laying out a set of the elegant Allan straight-link motion which these locomotives have. They were the last of many hundreds of saddle tank locomotives built at the Swindon factory.

Next comes a clutch of industrial locomotives belonging to the Society, reviewed in the order of gradually reducing association with the GWR. A point of psychological interest is that at this bottom level, names come back in again. *Trojan* is a saddle tank, built by Avonside in 1897, which came into the possession of the GWR in 1923 on absorption of the Alexandra Docks and Railway Co of Newport, receiving the number 1340. In 1932 No 1340 was sold to the Victoria Colliery Co of Wellington, Salop and via two other owners into the hands of the GWS in 1968. Another Avonside is 0–6–0 saddle tank *Pontyberem* of 1900 built as No 2 for the Burry Port & Gwendraeth Valley Railway and later sold to Mountain Ash Colliery in 1914, eight years before the little BP&GVR with its 15 locomotives was absorbed by the GWR. After being offered for sale by the NCB in 1970, it came into possession of the GWS and is now at Taunton.

Of the two remaining industrials, both 0–4–0 saddle tanks, the one at Taunton was at least built in GWR territory, being a product of Peckett's of Bristol, but neither they nor the two diesel shunters at Didcot add anything of significance to the locomotive collection. They are just useful.

Slightly irrelevant to this book are three major non-Great Western exhibits now at Didcot: 2–10–0 *Evening Star*, the last steam locomotive built at Swindon Works and for British Railways, is the largest; 4–6–2 *Winston Churchill* from the Southern Railway, but which drew the great man past Didcot on his last journey in 1965; finally, Hymek diesel No D7019, designed at Swindon for hauling trains over the lines of the Great Western's successor, the Western Region of British Railways. In 1972, the LNER class A2 4–6–2 *Blue Peter* came to Didcot for a brief period.

Lastly, there is on loan from the National collection since 1969 a venerable antique of great distinction and recently the oldest steamable locomotive in the Kingdom. This is *Shannon* alias *Jane*, an 0–4–0 well tank from the Wantage Tramway, built by George England of London as long ago as 1857. At the Shildon Rail 150 Cavalcade of 1975, *Shannon* was the oldest locomotive in steam by a margin of 20 years. When the tramway closed in 1946, she was bought for preservation by the Great Western Railway, thereby redressing by a small but appreciable amount the wrong done when *Lord of the Isles* was scrapped 40 years earlier. Before coming to Wantage in 1870 as No 5, the locomotive operated on the Sandy & Potton Railway in Bedford, for which it was built.

6 The Didcot carriage and wagon collection

If the outstanding feature of the standardised GWR twentieth century locomotive fleet was the technical restraint to which its perfection owed so much (although it perhaps bulged just a little towards the end) then by contrast the chief mechanical engineer's department sure let go when it came to carriages. Strangely enough, in the nineteenth century, the reverse was the case.

From the historian's point of view, of course, the frequent changes in design combined with many strange and often illogical quirks and complexities, present a fascinating study, but, one might add, a museum-keeper's nightmare. As we have seen, 30 items would give comprehensive cover to the locomotive fleet since 1900, but 300 would be more the mark to do the same for carriages. Did any other company, apart from the London & South Western on a limited scale, go to the trouble of building handed corridor brake thirds and composites so that, while the luggage compartments stayed at the outer ends and first class was kept together in the middle of a train, its corridors would elegantly keep to the same side, and then make nonsense of it all by becoming notorious for making up sets, even for important trains, from chosen stock chosen at random?

Didcot contains good examples of all but the two least important of the ten main carriage design families as will be described, and examples of most of the types except, notably, that GWR speciality the slip coach, and rather oddly a complete dining or refreshment car of any of the 26 varieties that there were. Incidentally, neither of the two missing links, the 'concertinas' of 1906–08 and the LMS-style 'low-waisted' design of 1936, can be seen elsewhere, nor can a slip coach of any company. As with the locomotives, a general description of the exhibits follows with numerical details in a table at the end of the chapter.

We must begin with the Clerestory Age, which contained

many non-clerestory coaches with plain flattish roofs and, of both of these types, the Didcot collection includes a modest offering. Of the non-clerestories of the period the Society has a rather nice pair of four-wheelers, a brake third of 1891, a six-wheel tri-composite of 1887 (the oldest carriage at Didcot) and an all-third of 1904. There is also a handsome passenger bogie brake built in 1898. The actual clerestory coaches that have survived to reach Didcot include two very basic non-corridor third class bogie coaches dating from 1901 and 1903. Restoration of these vehicles is involving major bodywork operations; all had been converted to departmental use by the removal of compartments etc.

Lest a false impression be given of the comforts offered in the clerestory age, it must be remembered that the coaches of this design family included such things as the vehicles of Britain's first corridor train, as well as the first dining, sleeping and 'seventy-foot' cars to run on the GWR. Recently the body of a clerestory composite dining car of 1903 has arrived at Didcot. The clerestory family salon of 1894 is interesting; the body was found near Reading with almost all internal furnishings complete, including the original upholstery, in spite of having been a residence for 40 years. Now that a suitable underframe has been found, the society has not only a lovely carriage but also a relic of those high and far off times when large families, complete with servants, dogs, trunks and luncheon baskets, travelled in one on their way to the Victorian equivalent of the Bahamas or Seychelles.

A single example of the carriages from the lines which were absorbed by the GWR in 1923 has come to Didcot. It is an ex-Cambrian Railways four-wheel tri-composite dating from 1895.

Like naval strategy, it was all-change with the coming of the Dreadnoughts in 1905. These vehicles at 73ft 6in long by 9ft 6in wide were too big to run on lines of any other company and not by any means small enough for the whole of the GWR. They were marked with a red triangle on the ends and an inscription 'NOT TO WORK ON THE EASTERN OR WESTERN VALLEYS LINES OR NORTH OF WOLVERHAMPTON AND HEREFORD'. No 3299 at Didcot not only represents the Dreadnoughts but also the whole unique GWR 70ft main-line fleet from the single clerestory vehicle to the last constructed during the bow-end period. Long carriages are yet another matter in which BR finds itself copying Western ideas of 70 years before. As on a present-day coach, the compartments of No 3299 are reached from the corridor, three cross-vestibules being provided. One quirk of the design is that the corridor crosses over at the centre; another is that there are no big windows.

After these magnificent vehicles and the brief un-represented concertina period (recessed doors gave the illusion of the concertina) came anti-climax in the form of the long and not too distinguished top-light era of 1908 to 1922. Undistinguished, that is, except for its variety which was fantastic, every imaginable type of coach being produced, frequently in both 70ft and 57ft varieties and sometimes in both left- and right-handed form. The coaches got their name from small rectangular extra windows provided between the roof line and the normal windows; it meant a 70ft corridor third having 147 windows. Understandably the toplights were blanked out in time but the name stuck. Steel panelling came in after the first world war, earlier coaches also acquiring this new feature in many instances.

A top-light corridor brake composite, a medical officer's saloon and two non-corridor brake thirds of this design family are at Didcot. The latter are interesting in that they have low roofs to run on the Circle line in London. Before 1939 one could catch a Great Western train (hauled by a Metropolitan electric locomotive) at, say, Liverpool Street, and find oneself in one of these actual vehicles, to run without change out into leafy Buckinghamshire, an example of one of the many conveniences of life that have vanished in the name of progress. These coaches ended their lives on miners' trains to Glyncorrwg, a line that also had clearance problems, but otherwise had little in common with London's Underground.

The bow-ended era (which, naturally, included flat-ended coaches and even some bow at one end and flat at the other) lasted from 1923 to 1932 and produced at least as great a variety as the top-light period. Bow-ends were actually introduced as part of a trial of the use of buck-eye automatic couplers and Pullman type vestibules, already standard on the East Coast route, to become standard on the Southern, and eventually on BR. Their main advantage lies in the reduction of the tendency for telescoping in an accident, but the GWR in the end preferred to spend its money on primary safety in the form of such things as cab signalling and getting the brakes on fast with quick-application valves. However, the bow-ended shape stayed on, reducing the length of corridor connections; it was even applied to non-corridor coaches with the unresolved dilemma of having either a strange bow-seat in the end compartments or a sealed new-moon shaped oubliette. Two bow-ended sets were built to 9ft 7in width in 1929 for the Cornish Riviera Express, receiving the accolade of the red triangle; incidentally that extra 7in made all the difference between a comfortable and an uncomfortable ride when seated four-a-side in corridor stock.

Five bow-enders of the plainer 60ft variety exist at Didcot to form a modest complete train (although such dull uniformity would be wholly untypical of the old company) and, although no diner could be provided, it might be finished off with a special kitchen-first-observation-saloon, originally for special parties, but latterly used by the general manager at Paddington.

Came the slump and GWR dividends dropping out of the sky to a paltry 3 per cent; this was reflected in the economy designs of 1934, with such austerities as abandonment of the bow-end, and fewer doors on corridor sides. One of these carriages was amongst the first vehicles to be restored at Didcot.

The following year, in contrast and to celebrate the centenary year, two of the least economically-designed train sets imaginable were built, as has been mentioned, for the now once more Limited Cornish Riviera. They followed the Dreadnought style in having no exterior doors to the compartments and in fact set the fashion for all subsequent GWR corridor coach construction. The only survivor is not in the possession of the GWS, but the Society does have three out of the eight super-saloons of similar basic design, constructed a few years before to provide Pullman-style accommodation on boat trains connecting with transatlantic liners calling at Plymouth – 'and save a day' as GW propaganda had it. Of course, all had the distinction of the red triangle mark since they were also 9ft 7in wide; they were the last to receive it.

Very briefly and most unusually, in 1936, the GWR found itself building almost exact copies (none of which have survived) of the current and very neat LMS low-waisted main-line coaches. This unusual course might have had something to do with the fact that Stanier, a Swindon man, now held the reins at Euston. Be that as it may, two years later coaches were coming out similar in concept but distinctive in design. These were the yellow disc stock of 1938–1941. The yellow disc sign fixed to their ends indicated that their profile allowed for country-wide working. This excellent and handsome group also appeared in great variety and, again, a modest clutch has been preserved by the Society, as listed. As always in times of stress and social change, officialdom and politicians find it even easier to get on our backs, so even in war-time special saloons had to be built for such people, at a time when ordinary men and women thought themselves lucky to find standing room on trains; one of these saloons now occasionally enhances the prestige of Didcot officialdom. An open excursion third class carriage of this yellow disc design was an early restoration at Didcot and the first to be allowed out into the world of diesel and electric British Rail.

The final design was the post-war Hawksworth steel-panelled stock – with domed *and* bowed ends – and the GWS has been able to acquire a corridor third, a brake composite and a 12-wheel sleeping car to this style which, in a train, broke up the roof line, in addition to the breaks in the body line characteristic of mixed groups of previous GWR stock. So the last CME, F. W. Hawksworth, could congratulate himself that he had added a whole new dimension to the traditional assymmetry that was the typical Western train.

For one particular purpose, the Great Western Railway was building to a design which, in contrast to the rest of its carriage fleet, had hardly changed from the beginning of the century. These were the specialised branch line and local train coaches which were quite unlike anything owned by the other companies. These vehicles, known originally as rail-motor trailers and later as auto-coaches, provided driving compartments from which the throttle of a suitably fitted steam engine as well as the train brakes could be controlled, thus avoiding the nuisance of the locomotive running round frequently on short distance workings. Large distinctive gongs were provided on the coach ends for warning purposes. The GWS has examples of the 1906, 1930 and 1950 buildings. The veteran of the three is known as 'the Ponderoza' on account of its 74ft length.

The GWR in the late 1930s pioneered the diesel railcar and the Society has one out of the 38 built, an example of the later trailer-hauling type. It should be noted that both the auto-coaches and the railcars were numbered in two separate series of their own.

One feature did, however, lift the appearance of the many unimpressive Great Western carriages out of the mediocre class and that is of course the outstanding style and quality of the beautiful chocolate and cream livery. This is again one of the many matters in which the GWS has followed the GWR in one of the very best of its traditions, and the Society's restored coach fleet is indeed a sight for sore eyes. In this connection, not yet mentioned is a pair of BR standard Mark I coaches still to be restored, obtained in fact to provide dormitory accommodation for volunteers. Certain Western features – such as bogies – were used in this very worthy design; the GWS Council might consider repainting them in the GWR colours that the Mark Is carried during the brave period of 1955–1960 when, like the Czechs and the Hungarians, Paddington defied the 222 Marylebone Road Kremlin in a hopeless attempt to be allowed to restore some of the old standards of service and esprit de corps.

For every 120 of the company's locomotives and every 425 of its carriages, the GWS has managed to preserve one and it is certainly as great an achievement, bearing in mind the indifference of the average enthusiast towards anything other than locomotives and coaches, to have done the same for one six-thousandth of the wagons. Without much first-hand knowledge, one has the impression that GWR wagons were sound, long-standardised and unspectacular. In an article published in *The Railway Magazine* during 1932, discussing the various wagons sent overseas during 1914–1918, a competent and involved observer (A. E. Sherington) judged the Swindon vehicles to have been the best without any question. The writer, involved (and complaining) about the de-Westernisation (if that is the word) of rail supply arrangements circa 1950, found that instead of rails flowing punctually and undamaged from the Steel Company of Wales on the Western's circuit-worked fleet of lovely vacuum-fitted 65ft GANE A rail wagons, they began arriving erratically – and often crippled – from the North East on dubious combinations of common-user single- and double-bolsters, originating from other companies.

To be fair, in recent years BR's own arrangements have now emulated those the GWR made for steel flows from South Wales 50 years earlier. In operational thinking, therefore, the GWR was also well in the van. Which brings us to the subject of wagon names, mainly for use on the telegraph, but in the case of any vehicle at all special painted on for identification. Choosing examples from amongst those preserved at Didcot, some were, like ASMO, made-up words; others referred to the cargo, eg FRUIT; CROCODILE suggested the look of the wagon, while

MICA and SIPHON were just nice aurally distinctive words chosen at random as names. Special instructions were written in handsome italic script; it is a lasting regret that Didcot's fleet does not include the PYTHON marked *Specially Strengthened for the Conveyance of Elephants*.

There was a nice social hierarchy, too, for the GWR was nothing if not a feudal railway. We have already dealt with the aristocracy, that is to say, the coach-built vehicles such as travelling post offices or full brakes finished in the full brown and cream livery. The six at Didcot are included in the list in chapter 20 under the carriage design family to which each belongs, but the remainder of the fleet, with few basic design changes to consider, can conveniently be dealt with type by type.

First came the so-called 'brown vehicles' which were those, although basically constructed like a wagon, having running gear suitable for passenger trains. A four-wheel FRUIT B van, a six-wheel prize cattle wagon and one of the famous bogie general purpose vans, SIPHON G, originally built for the now archaic idea of transporting milk in churns, are at Didcot. Representing the latest idea in milk transport, the latest that is before BR in recent years lost the business, is the GWR version of the freightliner wagon (again, 50 years ahead of its time) in the form of a ROTANK, a flat wagon for demountable milk tanks.

Of freight stock intended to run in freight trains, but of specialised type and therefore named, we have an ASMO four-wheel motor car van, CROCODILE F bogie and HYDRA D four-wheel well wagons. There is the equivalent of what the Americans call a *Reefer* in the form of the insulated MICA B van, a BLOATER fish van, a GRANO grain van and a TEVAN tea van.

Of standard GWR freight stock (and therefore named only in the telegraphic code book) there are five more vans, a shunter's truck and six open wagons; the latter includes an example of the brave attempt made by the GWR shortly before the second world war to introduce a fleet of modern high-capacity 20-ton coal wagons. One of the brake vans is the only real veteran in the collection, dating from 1894.

Service stock is well represented with tool and mess vans from both the Taunton and Penzance breakdown trains, now at Taunton and Didcot respectively. There is one steam and one hand crane and a sleeper wagon of the type named GRAMPUS in BR days.

7 Dart Valley railways

The formation and launching of the Dart Valley Railway Company presents the greatest possible contrast to the early efforts of the Great Western Society. Instead of a group of youngsters with then hardly a bent brass farthing to their names, we find a group of business and professional men, mostly from the Midlands, who had the means to set up a conventional limited company, with enough resources to purchase and equip a branch line.

Listen to Patrick Whitehouse, the first chairman of the DVR Co, defending the position in the short-lived but much lamented magazine *Steam Alive!*:

> The difference between the Dart Valley and the other preserved lines is that this railway has been acquired by a small commercial company, our view being that people get tired of endless appeals for money and that, in any case, the amount needed could not be raised that way.
>
> So the Company was formed and shares issued to anyone who felt they would care to participate. Suffice it to say that there was never any difficulty in raising the required sum and both large and small shareholders made up the participants in the Company. (There are no blocks of shares larger than 5% of the capital to be issued immediately). Not only that, but enthusiast involvement is encouraged by the recognised supporting organisation – the Dart Valley Railway Association, which is itself a large share-holder. We are now going forward together on this new adventure – as a tourist business not a transport organisation – but permanent staff and enthusiasts know that there is a great future ahead. The aim is 300,000 passengers in 1969. I think this will be met and continued.
>
> We are quite unashamed – we are out to make a profit as any good business should. Most of it will be ploughed back, but we are equally adamant that those who have supported us shall get a fair return on their money. Sometime during 1968 a letter from an enthusiast appeared in *The Railway Magazine* asking if it was generally known that there were people in railway preservation wishing to make a profit out of it. I hope that this will help to make it clear that there are but for a good reason – I believe Mr. Micawber had the answer, too. Fortunately, Dart Valley Railway Association members see the matter in its proper perspective and they are going from strength to strength.

Patrick Whitehouse bore the brunt of leading the

preservationist forces through the seven-year war against bureaucracy which lay between the first meeting to consider the idea and public operations on a portion of the company's chosen branch line. This chosen line, known prosaically in GWR days as the Ashburton Branch, was the one built and laid to Brunel's famous broad gauge by a company called the Buckfastleigh, Totnes and South Devon Railway. After the opening in 1872, the line quietly became part of the GWR in 1876, was changed to standard gauge in 1892 and for 66 years thereafter pursued an uneventful existence. The little passenger train (known locally as Bulliver) disappeared in 1958 and the line was closed to all traffic four years later, leaving a clear field to the railway preservationists.

When negotiations began, there seemed to be only one difficulty. At Totnes, the southern end of the branch, there were problems over the junction with the main line. Alas, the preservers have never, either then or since, been able to negotiate running powers into the BR station; present DVR trains stop in sight of it over the river, without even footpath access. So tantalising, particularly nowadays when Inter-City 125 trains from Totnes can set one down at Paddington in under 3 hours for the 202 miles.

But the delays were mostly caused by another problem, the last-minute refusal by the Ministry of Transport to allow British Railways to sell the northern $2\frac{1}{2}$ mile section between Buckfastleigh and the terminus at Ashburton, on the grounds that the land in question was needed for the reconstruction and doubling of the A38 Trunk Road. In some ways the result was an advantage because a $6\frac{1}{2}$ mile line would be likely to be that much more economic than a 9-mile one, but any true GW enthusiast must regret the loss of the station right in the centre of the pleasant country town of Ashburton, complete with its Brunel overall roof and small locomotive shed.

The collaborators – who must have been about to feel something of the sort of thrill that other railway pioneers would have felt during the mid-1800s in similar circumstances – were about to meet at the Turk's Head Hotel in Exeter (an excellent Railway Formation Tavern name) to take a formal decision to form their company when Pat Whitehouse received a letter from Bob Saunders, describing very vividly some rather sudden and inconsiderate rough-shod riding on the part of our top bureaucrats:

PERSONAL

Dear Mr. Whitehouse,

Dart Valley Railway
Totnes-Ashburton (closed) Branch

Since confirming our arrangements for the meeting at Exeter on the evening of the 28th January, we have received a very disturbing letter from the Ministry of Transport of which I should like you and Mr. Garland to be aware as it may well be necessary to further postpone our deliberation until we have been re-railed!

It is understood, confidentially, that an unexpected development occurred in the course of a meeting at Exeter on Monday (14th) between Western Region officials from Paddington and the Clerk and Legal Departments of the County Council who met to discuss the question of future liability for the public overbridges etc., situated on this branch and upon which, to a certain extent, the success of our negotiations depend.

Apparently towards the end of the meeting a representative of the Ministry of Transport arrived and tabled a copy of a letter addressed to us dated 10th January (of which a copy is enclosed) and indicated that the Minister proposed in the near future to open negotiations with British Railways to acquire that section of the branch between Ashburton and Buckfastleigh (2½ miles) for the purpose of constructing a diversion of the A38 trunk road!

This, I have ascertained, was the first intimation that Paddington had of any such proposal and I understand that County officials were equally surprised. It has certainly not come up in the course of our own discussion either with Paddington or with the County, and we have reason to believe that Paddington is as disturbed as we are by this late development. It is understood that they have requested the County officials to formally notify us of the Council's attitude to the proposals, and I have learned that the matter will be discussed by the Highways Committee later this month.

Mr. Stedman has formally acknowledged the letter pointing out the urgency for an early decision, and we have sent a copy to Paddington for their information, with a request for their observations, since it is probable that they will have to suspend negotiations until the position has been clarified by the M.O.T.

If the proposed diversion is not likely to be carried out for some years, as may well be the case, there seems no reason why the acquisition could not be dealt with when the time comes. The remaining 6½ miles Totnes to Buckfastleigh section would still be a worthwhile venture, and the estimates were based on the bulk of the traffic being carried between these points.

It is certainly a "bolt from the blue" and it is to be hoped that the reaction at Paddington will be to favour us with even more support for the preservation of at least part of the line. As a matter of interest it was only last week that a friend had lunch at Paddington with Mr. Fiennes, the General Manager and Mr. Sampson, and was told that they regarded the branch as one to be scheduled for preservation! I believe this also to be the view of certain interested County Council members, and our confidant there will ensure they are fully briefed.

We expect to hear further from Paddington in the next day or so and I will let you know not later than Wednesday if any useful purpose will be served by still meeting on the 28th January.

Yours sincerely,

(Sgd) Robt. J. Saunders

P.S. I have written similarly to Mr. Garland.

In fact the Dart Valley Railway Company Ltd did not begin its legal existence until 18 June 1965 and even then there was still the inevitable and lengthy grind of, first, standing by while British Railways changed the status of the line to a light railway; this was completed on 16 October, 1967. Then there followed the similar hassle of transferring the Light Railway Order from BR to DVR which eventually took place on 1 April 1969. All this accounted for the seven years that elapsed until re-opening day, 17 May, 1969, when the ceremony was performed by that arch-closer of railways, Dr Richard Beeching. One day in 1971, the company was allowed a final last day's running into Ashburton, before reconstruction of the A38 trunk road began.

Over the years the assets of the line have been enhanced by a magnificent restaurant and shop at Buckfastleigh, and, more recently, a locomotive repair shop of excellence and capability providing facilities second to none. There is also, under independent management, a miniature railway on surplus land beside the station. A crossing loop at Staverton was installed, but so far traffic has not risen to a point where it has really been needed.

The strange thing is that, just as worldly pressures and the need to survive changed Didcot into an operation run on strictly commercial lines, even if not for profit, the same forces have made the Dart Valley Company plough nearly every penny it earned back into the business rather than pay dividends to its enthusiast shareholders. On one occasion recently there was almost a riot at the Annual General Meeting, when the Chairman announced the payment of one. Put another way, having started at opposite ends of the commercial spectrum, both of these so different organisations find that the only way forward is along the same path.

Even so, the Dart Valley had, both literally and figuratively,

47

further to go; while Didcot closed down its satellites, the DVR acquired one that was to double the size of its operations. In 1972 British Railways announced the closure of its Torbay & Dartmouth line between Paignton and Kingswear; the DVR agreed not only to take it over but also continue regular year-round train services for school-children and shoppers.

The fairly heavy engineering works of the broad gauge Dartmouth & Torbay Railway, authorised in 1857, were not completed until 1864. From the beginning the line was worked by the South Devon Railway, so coming into the Great Western fold as a result of the Great Amalgamation of 1876; the D&T Company had previously lost its purely paper existence in 1872.

The line to Buckfastleigh follows the gentle and leafy valley of the Dart and, apart from one plain but beautifully situated iron bridge across the river, is devoid of any serious engineering works. The scenery is very nice, but not of the kind which is spelt with a capital S. The Torbay & Dartmouth on the other hand had to run diagonally across the grain of the terrain from the coast at Paignton to the tidal estuary of the Dart. The climb from Goodrington Sands, one mile south of Paignton is mostly at 1 in 71 steepening to 1 in 60. Side valleys are crossed on handsome arched masonary viaducts. The summit is reached at Churston, where the passing loop but not the junction has been restored. Shortly beyond comes Greenway tunnel. An exciting 1 in 66 descent follows, with occasional sudden views of the now wide Dart River below. As the name implies by the time Steam Ferry Crossing is reached, $5\frac{1}{2}$ miles from Paignton, the line has come down to a waterside location which it holds for the rest of the way to the terminus at Kingswear.

In addition, the Torbay line was not a branch but a main line, assuming that you define a main line as one that had regular year-round through trains to the nation's capital. While it would be nice to say that this was the first occasion on which a *main-line* railway was taken over by amateurs, most of the Dart Valley people were professionals.

This was one of the reasons why the transfer of the Torbay line from BR to the DVR took a fewer number of months than the original deal had taken years. For example, we find that BR received their Light Railway Order on 13 July 1972, while the transfer LRO became law on 8 November. The sale price was £250,000 plus £25,000 for track and signalling alterations.

The DVR took possession on 30 October, and chartered a BR

48

diesel service of four trains every weekday until the end of the year. On 1 January 1973 DVR began working the line itself with steam traction when the new track and signalling had been installed at Paignton. Substantial further capital had to be raised to produce the purchase money, but various properties included in the deal were in due time sold off and much of the sum expended recovered. The original intention to provide school trains and shopping services was found, not surprisingly, to be totally uneconomic; they were soon dropped and road services substituted. So the Torbay Steam Railway, as it was called at first, and later the Torbay & Dartmouth Railway, became wholly a summer season tourist operation.

In some ways the story could be said to end here. In their tourist guise the Buckfastleigh trains had got bigger and more varied than Bulliver had ever been, while those at Torbay, with the absence of such institutions as the daily Torbay Express (with Luncheon and Tea Car) to Paddington or the through trains to Manchester and Wolverhampton, have become a little less exciting.

There was of course much to do before the Company could get round to the installation of a useful passing loop (plus other facilities such as a new turntable) at Churston, the half-way point. Perhaps the most important building on either line to be constructed after the Torbay opening was the well-equipped repair shop at Buckfastleigh, formally opened in 1980; it goes a fair way towards solving the problem of keeping steam in action when the windfall of unused spare parts and partly-worn locomotives caused by BR's too rapid dieselisation policy finally becomes exhausted. But this is a matter for the next chapter.

One is left with a certain feeling that both the present day Dart Valley Railway operations are long in efficiency but a little short in *panache*. The management does rather seem to be in the position of someone with two theatres in the same street, who has Shakespeare playing at both of them; perhaps this is reflected in the annual passenger journeys which, currently at a level of 120,000 on the Buckfastleigh line, and 260,000 on the Torbay, seem less than the tourist potential of the area would indicate to be possible.

49

8 Dart Valley wheels

As we have seen in the last chapter, the Dart Valley Railway was conceived by a group of substance to keep alive that perfect thing, a Great Western West Country branch line. In obtaining motive power, the founders were in a position of having what they wanted, a pair of big, a pair of medium and a pair of small branch line engines, or in numerical terms, two 45XX 2–6–2Ts, two 64XX 0–6–0Ts and two 14XX 0–4–2Ts. The last two types were fitted for auto-train (push-and-pull) working and, among the rolling stock, the delightful and distinctive GWR auto-train trailers at first predominated. By a happy chance, of these three types the 64XX is not preserved at Didcot, nor are either of two very small pannier tank engine types of the 16XX and 1366 classes, examples of which arrived rather fortuitously on the property before opening day.

The first DVR locomotive, 2–6–2T No 4555, originally became the property of Patricks Garland and Whitehouse. It was the sixth of the 'gentleman's personal sporting locomotives' to be acquired by private individuals in Britain and the second Great Western one. Typically, in buying the locomotive, Pat Whitehouse did not deal with a clerk in the Stores Department, but with the Chairman of the Western Region Board. This was the late Reggie Hanks, who once issued an instruction that no British Railways (ie other than GWR) locomotive should be rostered for any train on which he was travelling! Reggie also had a steam fleet of his own and, to run it, a 'drive-yourself' live steam railway round the garden of his house at Oxford. Pat was then passed to Stanley Raymond, the General Manager at Paddington. For most people the General Manager is at a level one has to force one's way *up* to, if one wants to see him.

Raymond, later Sir Stanley Raymond, Chairman of British Railways, was very much against anything that smacked of keeping the past – even the lovely Bourne prints of the GWR in its earliest days were removed from the main corridor at

Above: Didcot develops I – Radstock signalbox re-erected in the Didcot complex, summer 1980. *Michael Baker*
Below: Didcot develops 2 – The carriage shed and traverser, January 1981. *Michael Baker*

Above: Didcot in broad gauge days on 27 September 1980! From left to right, a disc and crossbar signal, mixed gauge track using bridge rail on longitudinal timber baulks, the *Rocket* replica, and 'Mr Brunel'.
R. J. G. Antliff, courtesy GW Society
Below: The travelling Post Office in operation at Didcot, September 1980.
Courtesy GW Society

Paddington after he arrived there – but he regarded the sale of a tank engine as a mere commercial transaction. Later, when 4555 (which in fact had been working from Laira shed, Plymouth) had received attention at Swindon and was ready to be handed over, the Works Manager, Mr Ridgeway remarked 'you have some very powerful friends, Mr Whitehouse'.

With no sale of the Dart Valley as yet agreed, 4555 went to Tyseley Locomotive Depot in Birmingham; she paid for her keep by being used on local pick-up freight workings. On one famous occasion on the afternoon of 24 August, 1964, the engine of the Pines Express, no less, failed and like the Good Little Engine from a children's train book (which indeed she was and is) little 4555 was summoned to assist and was not found lacking. Coupled in behind another draftee, No 6991 *Acton Burnell Hall*, the 24 miles from Leamington to Snow Hill station, Birmingham, were run in 28 minutes, including the ascent of Hatton Bank. Those little 4ft 7½in diameter drivers must have spun like buzz-saws!

Further potential DVR shareholders bought the other locomotives. Industrialist John Wilkins acquired 0–6–0T 6435, while John Evans and Peter Stedman purchased 0–4–2T 1450. The two Pats were also responsible for 0–4–2T 1420, and 0–6–0T 6430 bought to provide spares but even now still practically intact although in dismantled kit form! Robin Butterell elevated himself from his usual miniature railway activities to raise money for, appropriately, one of the very small pannier tanks 0–6–0T No 1638. A tiny docks shunter (pannier tank 1369) also came, but this was a question of accommodating the owners rather than acquisition for use.

In due time all the locomotives were exchanged for shares, and once the line was running another 2–6–2T was bought. No 4588 came back from the dead at Woodham's yard at Barry in South Wales, and as an indication of the substance and standing of the DVR was put back into working order at BR's Swindon works. In a similar way all the other locomotives were restored professionally; this showed in the quality of the finish, which at that time was far above the standards achieved by most of the other preservers.

So far the DVR locomotive collection complemented that at Didcot by adding three new classes to those preserved; but subsequent acquisitions by the DVR Company itself (to cover the newly acquired Torbay line), by the Dart Valley Railway

Association and other individuals or groups with house room on the DVR has rather let the side down; the 13 locomotives in question only added *one* new GWR class, 52XX 2–8–0T No 5239. In fact, only three out of the 13 were of Great Western origin at all, the other two being 7827 *Lydham Manor* and 4920 *Dumbleton Hall*.

The clutch of five auto-trailers has been mentioned; all were examples of the last batches to be built, as late as 1951–1954. A fine collection of service saloons is interesting, including two engineers' saloons of 1896 and 1910, a directors' saloon of 1894 and the Dynamometer Car (for locomotive testing) of 1907. This vehicle has US-style domed ends to the clerestory, otherwise reserved for royal train carriages. Other vehicles duplicate items at Didcot, including two more 'super-saloons' *King George* (Dart Valley Association) and *Duchess of York*, (Dart Valley Company) two open excursion coaches of 1937 and a post-war brake composite. On the Torbay line, it is sad to relate, most passengers travel in BR standard stock, in GWR colours with DVR insignia, of which there are 13 items. Off the rails one notes a coach body thought to be of GWR origin dating from 1845.

The freight and service stock comprises 30 items, of which 26 are of GWR origin. The other items fresh to a student who has already studied the collection at Didcot, is a DAMO B motor car van, although the FRUIT and FRUIT D vans are a little different to the FRUIT B at Didcot. One steam and one hand crane are for use rather than admiration and, interestingly, there are on the books no less than 12 of the delightful Wickham motorised platelayers trolleys, of which the GWR was rather an addict.

In the museum is the most distinguished item of all, the one and only true survivor from the broad gauge. This is the little 'coffee-pot' (the nickname indicates the vertical boiler) locomotive called *Tiny*, which came into GWR hands via the equally tiny Torbay & Brixham Railway. *Tiny* was exhibited on the station platform at Newton Abbot for many years, but in 1980 was moved to Buckfastleigh where room indoors has been made available.

9 Narrow gauges

The 14 lengths of abandoned Great Western full-size road bed that have or are being put back into 'daisy-picking' use add up to around a respectable 3 per cent of the total; in contrast, of Great Western narrow-gauge road-bed (using the term in its post-19th century sense) some 70 per cent remains active, with some more being actively worked on for resuscitation. The premier amongst them is a real maverick, one that has more 'only's' to its name than any other, and had more than its fair share of troubles. This is the narrow gauge branch from Aberystwyth in mid-Wales, up the lovely Vale of Rheidol to the famous beauty spot known as the Devil's Bridge. Among a few of its 'only's' are the following:

Only GWR preserved line to use the same (and only the same) locomotives as in GWR days.

Only GWR preserved line to use the same (and only the same) rolling stock.

Only GWR preserved line to be used for the same traffic as before.

Only GWR preserved line to use solely steam traction, as well as the only purely pleasure line operated by the nationalised concern.

Only steam locomotives ever to bear the BR 'barbed wire' reversed arrows logo.

Everyone has a few subjects on which it is impossible to write objectively; for this writer this little gem of a railway is one of them. His first sight of it was on a clear September day in 1938 at the impressionable age of 15; of the train itself, it is enough to say that the GWR had (amazingly) just renewed all the carriages. Of the rest, everything was a little older but still maintained to superb main-line standards. As the little locomotive rolled along through the meadows soon after leaving Aberystwyth, the Rheidol line seemed pretty good, while the spectacular climb up the side of lovely Cwm Rheidol listening to the sharp and then beautifully-timed beat of the locomotive, was a turning point in an aspiring railway enthusiast's life.

The Vale of Rheidol railway was opened in 1902, mainly to serve some lead mines up the valley. The promoters were just too early for the Light Railways Act of 1896 and had their own Act, but in 1902 the line became 'light' legally as well as physically. The Rheidol line was a sound concept by any standards and, by the traditional ones of the narrow gauge, fantastic; shareholders actually received things called dividends. In 1900 this prosperity attracted a take-over by the Cambrian Railway, itself to be taken over (but not on account of its prosperity) by the GWR in 1922.

Among their new possessions, the Great Western management seem to have been rather intrigued by this tiny line; certainly they gave it their best, renewing immediately the motive power fleet by building two new locomotives and rebuilding one of the three others then existing, the other two (2–6–2T *King Edward* and 2–4–0T *Rheidol*) being scrapped. The Swindon 'Meccano Set' was stretched a little to produce these tiny iron ponies, but the cylinders at least were standard with the steam rail-motors of the time. From here they went on from strength to strength as has been described.

After the second world war (during which the line was closed) and nationalisation things went on pretty much as before until under a reorganisation the line was handed over from the Western Region to the London Midland. The people at Euston failed to realise, among other things, that this tiny line was showbiz not transport and, moreover, that it needed the same sort of care and love that amateur railwaymen further up the coast applied to their enterprises. In the end the hassle involved in running this remote tiny and uncloseable railway began to haunt BR's London Midland Region senior officials in a painful manner.

Looking for a way out, the LMR's General Manager asked Patrick Whitehouse of Tyseley and Dart Valley fame if he could find them a purchaser. A syndicate was formed with John Snell in the pilot's seat (but including this writer among others) and negotiations began; they were approaching conclusion with a sale price almost agreed in the £22,000–£25,000 region, when an ill-advised local press release was made. Pressure from local members of the locomotivemen's union then resulted in the Minister of Transport forbidding BR to go ahead with the sale.

With hindsight it would seem that a *fait accompli* might just have carried the day.

But from the point of view of the GWR preservationist, one advantage has resulted from this failure; the promoters had in mind expanding operations with foreign stock. Indeed, two neat little 0–8–0s were bought from lines in East Germany to Britain and nothing could be less Great Western than this pair. So the enchanting Rheidol soldiers on; to prevent destruction of the Valley's forests by fire, all three locomotives have been converted to oil burning and the terminus at Aberystwyth has been altered, but otherwise it is the only bit of God's Wonderful Railway that remains as it was before the Fall.

The Light Railways Act came just in time for the nine mile narrow-gauge line built to connect Welshpool with Llanfair Caereinion to become the 2ft 6in gauge Welshpool & Llanfair Light Railway, authorised in 1898. The Cambrian Railways took it over after the opening in 1903 and in 1922 the line passed to the GWR.

The two excellent Beyer-Peacock 0–6–0Ts *The Earl* and *Countess*, named after the Earl and Countess of Powys, whose seat was (and is) nearby and who had played a large part in promoting the line, needed little beyond nice brass safety valve covers to bring them up to Swindon standards, unlike so much material that was absorbed into the old company. Some new freight rolling stock appeared, while passenger operations (their scale may be judged from the fact that there were only three passenger cars) ceased in 1931.

So the little line continued to serve the farmers of the pleasant Banwy Valley. When in 1956 its usefulness had come to an end, the Western Region of British Railways quietly and painlessly leased it to a small group of enthusiasts who wanted to run the line as a tourist railway for what were then non-existent tourists. Since the line already operated on a Light Railway Order, another one, in fact dated 3 October 1962, transferred the powers to the lessors. The complex two-stage process referred to in the case of other transfers was not necessary for this one.

What has happened at Llanfair is what no doubt would have occurred on the Rheidol line had BR been allowed to sell it as they wanted, that is, the almost complete superseding of GWR equipment by others. As regards locomotives currently on the property, the proportion of them that are ex-Great Western has fallen from 100 per cent to 10 per cent in the 20 years of Society

57

presence. Even so, who would have dreamed that trains from such far-off places as Austria, South Africa, Barbados and Sierra Leone would have been seen on GWR metals? No ex-GWR carriages were ever involved, but some freight wagons (3 open, 2 vans, 1 cattle truck, 2 brake vans) survive in service use.

At the time of writing, opening of the final section to Raven Square on the outskirts of Welshpool is imminent. For obvious reasons the section through the town to the BR station, where the housewives had to take their washing in to allow trains to pass, and which also had such delights as a blind ungated level crossing over the main road, was never handed over to the Society. The fact that it has taken so long for the preservers to attain their objective is a reflection of prudent management and a patronage whose growth has been slow but sure; in 1980 this amounted to 75,000 passenger journeys.

The third Great Western narrow-gauge line (although perhaps one should say 'less than 4ft $8\frac{1}{2}$in', for in true GWR terms narrow gauge means 'less than 7ft $0\frac{1}{4}$in') was the one that got away. The little 2ft 3in gauge Corris Railway, which ran $6\frac{1}{2}$ miles (with $4\frac{3}{4}$ miles of branches) from Machynlleth up the attractive Corris Valley to serve slate mines, as well as the villages of Corris and Aberllefenni came into GWR hands in a strange manner via the Bristol Tramways & Carriage Company. The takeover was a kind of return deal when in the 1920s the main line railways were forced by a particularly ill-advised piece of legislation to dispose of their passenger road-motor interests.

Just as happened over the Welshpool line, the GWR continued to run the Corris. But then in 1948 a river spate swept away the bank of the Afon Dyfi at the point where the Corris line crossed the river, and that was the end of the line. In 1951 the two Corris locomotives found a home on the nearby Talyllyn Railway then pioneering railway preservation. They were offered to the infant Talyllyn Society at the generous price of £25 each; the engines in question were Hughes 0–4–2T No 3 of 1878 (now known as *Sir Haydn*) and Kerr Stuart 0–4–2T No 4 of 1921, now called *Edward Thomas*.

A small group of enthusiasts with few resources beyond strong arms and stout hearts known as the Corris Railway Society is bravely attempting to restore a short length of the upper end of the line, from Maespoeth (where the old locomotive shed still stands) to Corris village itself. This is a section where, exceptionally, the line does not run alongside a busy main road.

The saying 'It's dogged as does it' applies with great force to railway preservation and it may well be that the Society will overcome the many problems which exist, in this case particularly accentuated over recent years by raging inflation and the small number of members who participate. Several years' fund-raising has left them with more money to find than when they began.

In addition to these sections of the Great Western which were originally narrow gauge, some other sections of GWR road-bed have been put back into railway use with narrow-gauge rolling stock, almost none of it Great Western in origin. On the other hand these schemes all make use of GWR buildings and structures to a greater or lesser extent. The Bala Lake Railway runs $4\frac{1}{2}$ miles from Llanuwchllyn GWR station to a new halt close by the old Llangower station; motive power is by new diesel locomotives or, on high days and holidays, restored Hunslet 0–4–0Ts which once worked in the Dinorwic slate quarries.

The Brecon Mountain Railway was opened in 1980 over the two miles from Pant (change for Dowlais) to Ponsticill Junction (change for Merthyr) a section of the road-bed of the old Newport & Brecon line. It is the first stage of an elaborate scheme to run $5\frac{1}{2}$ miles of slim gauge track up to and beyond the summit tunnel of this spectacular line. Steam motive power under restoration includes a big Baldwin 4–6–2 and a huge 2–6–2+2–6–2 Garratt, both from South Africa.

The Welsh Highland Railway Preservation Society also reopened a section of line approximately $\frac{3}{4}$-mile long in 1980, announcing the deed as a first restoration of the original WHR. Not so, of course; the section opened was on the course of an ex-Cambrian Railway (and hence ex-GWR) siding at Porthmadog. On the other hand, among its vehicles can be found a genuine product of Swindon, a tiny passenger train brake van from the Vale of Rheidol line.

Exceptionally in this list, neither of two-foot-something gauge nor situated in Wales, is a line in miniature form. The two mile 15in gauge line (using light-alloy rails!), known as the Lappa Valley Railroad, has been laid down on a stretch of the old Newquay to Perranporth line between Benny Mill Halt and a leisure centre at the East Wheal Rose mine site. Steam and internal-combustion traction is employed.

One must just mention an ephemeral 2ft gauge line which appeared for a brief season in the late 1970s at Dinas Mawddy not far from Corris. It followed the course of the old Mawddy Railway for a short distance and used a small newly-built steam locomotive.

As regards future proposals, one still under consideration is the Vale of Teifi Railway, to be laid on part of the Pencader to Newcastle Emlyn branch. Finally, there is the Festiniog Railway, which is likely to make use of a few yards of ex-GWR roadbed when it finally reaches the town of Blaenau Ffestiniog in 1982. On it will be laid the platform lines of the new million-pound railway station now under construction in the centre of the town.

10 The Tyseley story

The story of what is now called the Birmingham Railway Museum, adjacent to the British Rail motive power depot at Tyseley, is very much the story of one man's contribution to railway preservation. Patrick Whitehouse's name has been mentioned several times in this narrative; for example, in taking a leading role in such pioneer enterprises as the Talyllyn Railway Preservation Society and the Dart Valley Railway. However, Tyseley was and is his child and his child only; his was the drive that brought it into being and his the guidance and *savoir faire* that has been (and is – even though on paper he no longer plays an executive role there) shaping the organisation to suit changing pressures and circumstances.

Tyseley, $3\frac{1}{4}$ miles south of the Great Western Railway's Snow Hill station had been the site of Birmingham's principal GWR locomotive depot since 1908. This was the time when most of the stations and lines in the area had been enlarged in anticipation of increased traffic following the opening of the new short route to London via High Wycombe. In the years before steam traction came to an end, over 100 steam locomotives were allocated there. On the whole they were a rather less glamorous group than the much smaller number there today, since the Castles (and also the Kings) that hauled the main Birmingham to Paddington expresses lived at Stafford Road, Wolverhampton or Old Oak Common, London. There was some express work, though, on the smartly-timed and energetically-run Birmingham to Cardiff trains both via Stratford-upon-Avon and via Worcester, and these were protected by a dozen or so Hall class 4–6–0s. The Birmingham suburban services were in the hands of some 30 51XX 2–6–2Ts, while shunting and trip work in the Black Country was done by a fleet of 40 57XX 0–6–0Ts. In small numbers were Granges, 2251 class 0–6–0s, 43XX 2–6–0s, Manors, Dukedog 4–4–0s and ROD 2–8–0s as well as 28XX 2–8–0s.

To carry out intermediate repairs on this collection was a repair shop or factory adjoining the roundhouse and it was in here that a corner was found for 2–6–2T No 4555 while she waited to go to the Dart Valley line. Later, other DVR locomotives joined her and room was found for them in the running shed.

Mention has already been made of the famous commemorative run of 9 May, 1964 on which *Pendennis Castle* disgraced herself by dropping some firebars. Another of the three Castles which had been specially selected and prepared for this run was No 7029 *Clun Castle* (the third was No 5054 *Earl of Ducie*). No 7029 brought the train back from Plymouth to Bristol, running the $129\frac{1}{2}$ miles in the remarkable time of 133 minutes, including 92mph on the level near Nailsea. The flagrant disregard of speed limits between Plymouth and Exeter that enabled *City of Truro* to do the same run in 14 minutes less in 1904 was not, one is thankful to say, a feature of the day's enjoyments.

Two gentlemen from Cornwall, John Trounson and John Southern (who now has a superb Railroad Park right in the centre of GWR territory near Liskeard) got up a fund to preserve *Clun Castle*, which was withdrawn at Gloucester shed on 31 December, 1965 and set aside for the preservers. Even so, insufficient cash had been raised and the organisers approached the Dart Valley Railway, which seemed in the foreseeable future to be the only possible likely location connected to but not part of BR. Patrick Whitehouse and John Evans produced the remaining funds needed, so obtaining a controlling interest. Since the DVR line was not then in possession of the DVR Co, *Clun* went to Tyseley and during 1966 was used on a number of steam excursions.

Later John Evans sold out his share and, now in sole control, Pat Whitehouse had the locomotive restored to GWR colours. This task absorbed some 350 man-days of labour. Swindon's own lining-out specialist even came up to do the lining and lettering and he insisted that the full GREAT WESTERN title be used, a livery that had not been seen in normal service since the adoption of the circular monogram in 1935. No 7029 has held to this superb style ever since, in spite of some criticism in the railway press that it was one she had never borne in service. One famous *Clun* outing marked the end of through services on the old Great Western line between Paddington and Birkenhead via Birmingham (Snow Hill), which coincided with the start of electric operation between Birmingham and London (Euston). On 4 March, 1967, Ian Allan Ltd, chartered two steam-hauled specials over the old route; between Banbury and Chester the first was hauled by *Clun Castle*, *Pendennis Castle* being used for the second from Didcot. Alas, it was *Clun*'s turn to disgrace herself. On the return journey, a lock-nut which secured the connection between one of the rocker arms and the valve of one of the outside cylinders, loosened and put the valve timing seriously out. The locomotive was able to complete the journey, but the incident brought home to the owner the sort of problem he would have to face in the future.

A man called Jim Kent, a lecturer in mechanical engineering at Warley Technical College, was on the trip yard and hearing (literally) of this happening, offered his services. Jim is a superb engineer, the original complete perfectionist as well as a man of few words, but when he says something, he means it. Since 1967 he has spent an untold number of hours at Tyseley repairing and rebuilding the numerous mountains of scrap metal which are still being presented to him for attention. Even more important, he has managed to set up a complete armoury of the tools for the job, including such heavy artillery as a wheel lathe and a wheel-drop, capable of handling those mighty wheels up to 7ft diameter, articles which have no counterpart on the modern railway.

Although Tyseley was also to go in for steam locomotives from Birmingham's other railway, Jim's appreciation of fine mechanical engineering means that he very much prefers working on the GWR engines there, on account of the superior workmanship and accuracy that went into their building. It is true that people are apt to refer to *Clun Castle*, as *Clunc*, but this is like the big man who is known to his friends as 'Tiny'. A combination of Swindon design and Kent maintenance has made this particular locomotive one of the least liable to clunking in the world.

Non-GWR partisans often feel incensed by the claim that the Great Western built its locomotives better — a similar sort of antipathy that one feels towards anyone who claims any form of moral superiority. Of course, it is not a moral question but one of deliberate choice; accuracy is expensive and it is very much a matter of opinion whether the cost was worth while. The Swindon authorities did think so and, as related in K. J. Cook's presidential address of 1955 to the Institution of Locomotive Engineers entitled 'The Steam Locomotive – Machine of Precision', they set themselves up with the kit to do it. As regards skill, it probably needed more to attain the modest standards of accuracy typical of other works with string lines, centre-pops and scribed lines, than the very high Swindon standards of using such devices as their Zeiss optical measuring equipment. Even so, the story that British Rail standards for fits and tolerances for a locomotive when new corresponded to Swindon's for one when it was worn out was only a modest exaggeration.

So two men of determination now held the reins at Tyseley, both very able in their own particular spheres. Through his friendship with many of the BR top brass, Pat was able to arrange for *Clun Castle* to travel far and wide, even in places were Castles had never previously been, such as Newcastle-upon-Tyne. This was part of a series of excursions arranged by Gerard Fiennes, General Manager of the new combined Eastern and North Eastern Region. During his sojourn in charge at Paddington, Gerry had been very much the driving force behind the high-speed 'City of Truro Commemoration' excursion of 1964. As he relates in his entertaining autobiography, *I Tried to Run a Railway* he was at that time very much at odds with the policies and attitudes of the central management of British Railways; it does seem as though this invitation for *Clun Castle* to run on the Eastern Region was a deliberate act of defiance against the BR Board, in respect of its declared policy of discouraging nostalgic operations such as steam-hauled specials; it was a monumental Marylebone-Road-tease if you like.

Be that as it may, *Clun* was stationed at Peterborough for a period in the autumn of 1967 and worked several special trains over the Eastern Region. King's Cross to Leeds was the first task to be tackled, marking the occasion 40 years before when *Pendennis Castle* herself demonstrated a considerable superiority both in coal consumption and in performance over the native Flying Scotsman-type Pacifics. A run to Carlisle and back via Leeds on 30 September and 1 October put GWR motive power over both Shap and Ais Gill Summits, but it was marred on the return journey by a vicious attempt at sabotage. Quantities of cotton waste were put in the tender, putting both injectors out of action. A paragraph appeared in *The Railway Magazine* for December 1967 suggesting that private locomotive owners should fit padlocks to the covers of the water fillers on their tenders! Happily, occurrences of this kind have not proved a problem over the years; the only recurring trouble has been when mentally unbalanced enthusiasts of the kind the Cause could well do without, grease the rails ahead of steam excursions so that they should slip spectacularly to a standstill.

Even so, the Eastern Region operations of *Clun Castle* were a three-way success – excellent publicity for all concerned, as well as some very welcome and timely extra finance for both BR and for *Clun*'s owners. After all expenses had been met, *Clun Castle* earned £3,000 in the pounds of those days; this then quite handsome sum was enough to pay for the conversion of the covered coaling stage at Tyseley to a two-road locomotive shed, as well as the purchase of a treasure house of spare parts and tools. In principle, too, this surplus seemed to demonstrate – as it turned out quite falsely – that private steam excursions could finance the continued maintenance and repair work needed to keep private steam locomotives in operable condition.

All this was made necessary and, indeed, became possible when Tyseley motive power depot was closed to steam. A new diesel depot was built and the steam shed demolished, leaving the preserved locomotives without a roof over their heads. However, the basis of one existed in the now redundant coaling stage; this was fortunately situated in a part of the old depot which was neither needed for the new diesel depot nor near the main road and so a candidate for a profitable sale. There was enough room on the upper coal-heaving storey for two 4–6–0s to be kept under cover, and space beneath for storage of those spare parts and tools. But it was for a short time only that Tyseley functioned in the way its originators intended as a private steam locomotive depot, with enough revenue coming in to ensure the continued existence in good shape of the two members of its fleet. It also managed to pay dividends and salaries to those who gave their money and time to the project in the form of pleasure; imagine the reward – quite beyond the power of money to buy – of riding *Clun Castle* as she pounded up the famous Long Drag, when crossing the Pennines on the run between Leeds and Carlisle. Such an arrangement had the happy result of attracting professional helpers from among the drivers and firemen of the old depot; one of the earliest was Bernard Rainbow. Bernard was another of several who put in an immense number of voluntary hours at Tyseley, over and above those occupied by an exacting job; in due course he became the depot's Superintendent of Operations.

But, alas, the hopes of those who had built up this neat depot seemed doomed, when, on 4 August 1968, normal steam operation came to an end on British Railways, and the BR Board finally imposed an absolute ban on the movement of any locomotive in steam on its standard gauge line. There was one exception, 4–6–2 *Flying Scotsman*, for the running of which owner Alan Pegler had a binding and specific contract. In fact, the Tyseley organisation had a letter of intent from BR regarding continued steam operation there, but it was thought prudent to heed a hint that an attempt to treat this as legally binding would lead to withdrawal of the co-operation which this infant private depot badly needed at that period.

From a material point of view the next decade was one of steady progress and improvement. A new ground-level repair shop and running shed was built; the installation of such major items as the wheel lathe and wheel-drop also involved major civil engineering. A number of further locomotives (mostly Great Western) were purchased. Three further Castle class locomotives were obtained from Woodham's scrapyard at Barry. No 7027 *Thornbury Castle* came from the same building lot as *Clun*, but it was never fitted with the double chimney and so the two locomotives make an interesting comparison. Two others, No 5043 *Earl of Mount Edgcumbe* (built in 1936 and originally named *Barbury Castle*), and No 5080 *Defiant* (built in 1939 as *Ogmore Castle* and renamed in 1941) were bought in order to provide spare parts for No 7029 and to assist in the restoration of No 7027. One major part needed was a pair of outside connecting rods and these large specialist items had to be obtained from elsewhere; it is an illustration of how those at Tyseley go about their affairs that an order was properly placed with one of the very few steam locomotive works left in the world, Chitteranjan in India. When delivered they proved to be fully up to the most exacting Kent-Swindon standards and, rather ironically, the ship carrying them passed not far from the Suez Canal, one going the other way with No 4079 *Pendennis Castle* on board as we shall see later.

To represent true Tyseley classes, 4–6–0 No 4983 *Albert Hall* was bought (its restoration is now well advanced) and straight out of service with London Transport came 57XX 0–6–0 Pannier Tanks Nos 7752 and 7760 (LT 94 and LT 90 respectively). No 9600 of this class came from the National Coal Board and is presently being overhauled. Finally two more hulks from Barry, 56XX 0–6–2T No 5637 and 51XX 2–6–2T No 4160 arrived, with a view to restoration in the long term.

Other GWR vehicles include two modern saloons, semi-royal saloon No 9001 and engineer's inspection saloon No 80972, two FRUIT D vans, two standard five-plank wagons, a box van, a six-ton hand crane and the inevitable TOAD goods brake van. As well as these major exhibits, what is now a museum hall as well as a running shed and repair shop contains many smaller GWR items of interest and rarity.

Which brings us to another point, the sad fact that the financial story of Tyseley has far from matched the tale of material achievement there. Even so, the large amount of capital needed for the venture has been found not exactly easily, but at least with results commensurate with the extraordinary efforts made and the heavy-calibre guns employed in the raising of it.

In other ways, however, the results have not been commensurate with the effort. The problem has lain in the fact that, in spite of so much able voluntary help, that even 'taking one year with another' (as for BR) it has not been possible to meet the day-by-day running expenses with the receipts from the centre's activities. As described elsewhere, when steam excursions returned to BR in 1970, they soon involved the steam owners in a scale of expenditure that left little over from (and often did not even meet) the direct costs of the outing. The contrast between the high price charged to railway lovers (who respect the insides of the carriages and provide their own locomotive) and the low one charged to football fans (who habitually wreck the coaches and need a locomotive provided for them) is just one of those absurdities of management that makes one despair for the future of railways in this country.

From the first, open days were regularly held at Tyseley. Some were very ambitious with locomotives and trains and other attractions brought from all over the country; others merely involved the native inhabitants. Hazards included the possibility of being rained off, and even if fine the dust of the grassless Tyseley terrain was a discouragement unless the day was also calm. There was also the problem that in due time Birmingham railway enthusiasts had seen all that Tyseley had to offer several times; furthermore, the locality, poised between the inner and outer suburbs of the city, while very convenient for those who worked there, was not one to attract families for a Sunday out.

On occasions the Tyseley 'circus' went abroad, notably to Allerton, Liverpool and Cricklewood, London. A big diesel locomotive set off with an amazing train which included three 4–6–0s in light steam for lubrication purposes. As an indication of the childish and emotional response to these steam operations at headquarters, instructions were issued for stops to be bolted to the regulator quadrants of each engine so that the throttles could not be opened wide enough to provide traction. The steam owners were delighted that on the first outing the diesel stalled on the incline leading out of Tyseley depot; the throttle stop on the author's locomotive, *Eric Treacy*, had to be removed and the caravan steamed out of trouble. The stop was not replaced.

In this way *Clun Castle* travelled over several more lines where no Castle class had been before and on arrival worked trains over long sidings or freight loops adjacent to the motive power depot visited. It was a period when the thin end of the wedge had been inserted and steam haulage was allowed on other than sacred running lines, usually involving a steam locomotive at each end of the train. Similar arrangements applied at home during open days there.

The situation has been made worse by the fact that costs have risen, not only in line with inflation but in real terms as well. For example, after a boiler flue accident which occurred at Didcot in 1977, plus another incident elsewhere, it was considered prudent that boiler work at Tyseley should be done by a professional, and the only way to obtain such services was to have a paid boiler-smith full-time on site.

One way in which a subsidy could be obtained was by interesting the civic authorities of the City of Birmingham in the project. The Museums Department of the City already had some stuffed-and-mounted railway locomotives in their care. As a result, Tyseley (as this museum-depot will always be known to railfans everywhere) changed its official name from the Standard Gauge Steam Trust to the Birmingham Railway Museum. Other behind-the-scenes legal instruments in use at Tyseley include 7029 Clun Castle Ltd and Albert Hall Ltd, but these are not used publicly. Even so, the problem is not fully solved and so a further possibility is being considered by which the depot should become in some way an out-station of the National Railway Museum. The York museum has accepted the task of maintaining full-size steam locomotives in running order

68

Above: Didcot on 1 December 1979 with No 7808 *Cookham Manor* on No 8 road. *P. C. Treloar*
Below: Didcot open day in September 1978 with 0-6-0 pannier tank No 3738 and 0-6-0 saddle tank No 1363 performing on the demonstration line. *Michael Baker*

Above: Naming ceremony 1 - Mrs Una Mynors, owner of locomotive No 5051, unveils the nameplate *Drysllwyn Castle* at Didcot railway centre on Easter Saturday 1980. On her right is Graham Perry, chairman of the Great Western Society. *Courtesy GW Society*

Below: Naming ceremony 2 – Earl Bathurst unveils the nameplate *Earl Bathurst* on the other side of No 5051 at Didcot on Easter Saturday 1980. Notice that the nameplate is an exact replica of the original made to fit the smaller diameter splasher of the Earl class 4-4-0s which means that the plate is not concentric with the curve of the splasher. *Courtesy GW Society*

yet it has none of the heavy machine tools needed for the job. The skills and machinery available at Tyseley would fulfil a very real need for York, while the possibility of having a wide choice of exhibits would be an advantage for Tyseley. It is not to be imagined that the priceless and unmatched facilities at Tyseley for keeping steam in being for future generations could ever be lost.

11 Bulmers of Hereford

Since this discussion of GWR preservation has as its basis the collection of the private and voluntary Great Western Society, it is strange to relate that the biggest gap in that collection is filled by a firm which entered locomotive madness from wholly commercial motives – in fact, purely as (in the best sense of the term) an advertising stunt. Nevertheless, the honourable name of H. P. Bulmer & Co, Cider Makers, of Hereford is one that all good GW men and true have reason to venerate for two great things they did for the Cause. It turned out like this . . .

We are now talking, of course, of the most famous of all GWR locomotives, No 6000 *King George V*, the prototype of its class and indeed (as the GWR *Boys of All Ages Book* put it) the 'King of Railway Locomotives'. Speaking as a Great Western civil engineer, your author is proud to relate that the genesis of the Kings has much to do with the far-sightedness of his department long before. Railway civil engineering is such a long-term business that those in charge of it find themselves habitually looking well into the future. In doing so it is no use asking those who run the trains what will be their requirements say 20 years ahead; operating departments are notorious in, say, the mornings for concerning themselves (often not too effectively) only with 'adhocery' connected with the afternoon's trains. So, when in the mid-1920s it became apparent that heavier locomotives were needed to work the principal GWR trains, the chief (civil) engineer was in the strong position of being able to say, as it were, that 'we thought you might be going to ask that'; for many past years all renewals had allowed for a 22-ton axle load instead of the current previously 20-ton limit.

Hence a 10 per cent enlargement of a Castle could be allowed and this is really what the Kings were. Oddly enough there was already a King class on the Great Western, – one batch of the Stars, if you like a 5 per cent *reduction* on the Castles – and these became Monarchs. Alas, nearly all the 10 real Monarchs so honoured blotted their copybooks one way and another and in the end only the first engine, No 4021 *British Monarch* survived the war to withdrawal with name intact. Incidentally, the civil engineer's pre-vision obviated any need for a possible eight-coupled GWR express locomotive; for some speculations on the form one might have taken, the reader is referred to the late Professor Tuplin's three fascinating books on the best of all subjects, *Great Western Steam, Great Western Power, Great Western Saints and Sinners,* all published by George Allen & Unwin.

In general the design followed the gospel as laid down by Churchward, but in order to provide clearance between the front wheels and the enlarged inside cylinders, the new locomotives had the unique bogie with outside front and inside rear bearings. This distinctive feature is the trade mark of the Kings; it was made to stand out even more by extra coil springs added after No 6003 had put a leading pair of wheels on the floor near Midgham on what was nearly the locomotive's first revenue trip; this occurred when hauling the Limited, no less. *King George V* put in only a very brief period of service before visiting America to take part in the centenary celebrations of the Baltimore & Ohio Railroad. The locomotive came back from the USA with medals, a presentation bell and much honour, as well as the modified spring arrangement made and fitted in the B&O shops.

As is well known, in service the 30 Kings were very successful; the main improvements made over *KGV*'s years of service comprised the provision of high superheat and mechanical lubrication (in April 1952) and double chimney and blastpipe provided in December 1956. It was in this form that the engine was withdrawn on 3 November, 1962, having on its last day of service stood in successfully for a failed diesel on the Inter-City Limited, one of BR's most important trains.

There was never any argument that *King George V* should be preserved; the only question was where? After being held at Swindon for a time during 1964, No 6000 was towed to Stratford in East London as a preliminary to becoming a permanent 'stuffed and mounted' exhibit in the railway museum at Clapham. In the event Clapham ceased to have a future as the National Railway Museum and on New Year's eve 1966 *KGV* was towed back to Swindon. The locomotive was placed in the stock shed there under the trusteeship of Swindon Corporation, with a view to eventual display in the Borough, although nothing could be done at once because their excellent Great Western Museum was already full and financial stringency precluded any extension.

This is where H. P. Bulmer & Co entered the scene; Peter Prior, its energetic Managing Director, was looking for some novel instrument of publicity for his firm's highly recommended products. He already had a private siding and was in the process of acquiring a train of Pullman Cars from the Golden Arrow express. These were to be used as a reception centre for visitors to the factory in the summer and at other times to serve as a cider exhibition train for touring the country. Following a casual meeting and a quite un-casual conversation with some unknown fellow first-class passenger and GW enthusiast on the train between Hereford and Paddington, Peter realised that he had found what he wanted, the most famous locomotive of Hereford's own railway. What I think he did not realise was that Love for Steam at that time, so far as BR was concerned, was Love In A Cold Climate.

An acceptable arrangement was reached with Swindon Corporation almost at once, but as regards BR it was a very different story. Major obstacles were continually put in the way of the project and, for once, the King enthusiasts (who did not want the locomotive to leave Swindon) and the top brass of BR at 222 Marylebone Road were allies. The view at the very top – seen from your author's viewpoint, at the time a humble desk on the attic floor of No 222 – was the reasonable if misguided one that any steam operations tended to detract from their wished-for image of BR as a go-ahead modern industry. Immediately below the very top there was such an unthinking and passionate anti-steam attitude that one can only surmise the true reason and is forced to conclude that those concerned were in the position of selfish children who hated the idea of someone else playing with their train set. Happily more reasonable views now prevail but at the time the emotional response seemed almost past belief.

Not everyone at BR's HQ felt this way and an opportunity occurred with the passing of the 1968 Transport Act. A provision of this Act was the approval for and encouragement of what was called diversification, that is the use of BR's facilities for things other than transport. A group of members of the planning department were called together by Kenneth Smith (then Chief Planning Officer) to suggest ideas for investigation. A half-serious suggestion that there was money to be earned in steam entertainment met with the wholly acceptable response 'Brian, when can we have your paper on the subject?'. When finished this document (see Appendix) was put to the Board and, to the surprise of its unwitting sponsor, produced some quite disproportionate heavy-calibre return fire from certain of the members. Nevertheless, it was the only one of the new ideas put forward at that time under diversification which came to fruition in the end.

Meanwhile Peter Prior was on the assault course. The first obstacle put in his way was the removal of track leading into the shed where No 6000 was standing. His reply was to have the track relaid temporarily by Bulmer's own contractors; the next hurdle was that BR was then not prepared to allow one of its shunting engines to run on it. Even if this could be overcome there was to be a vicious temporary connection charge amounting to the equivalent of over £10,000 in today's money. In the end the money was paid and the engine hauled out on to BR's metals manually by a huge volunteer force pulling on ropes tug-of-war fashion. With the Mayor and Mayoress of Swindon standing on the front buffer beam, the publicity obtained turned out to be good value, so everything turned out right in the end, both for Bulmers and (in spite of themselves) for BR.

Again a prohibitive price was put upon the towing operation from Swindon to a firm (A. R. Adams & Son of Newport) in South Wales for overhaul and then on to Hereford. Arrangements were made locally for the journey from Newport to Hereford to be made appropriately behind diesel-hydraulic *Western Monarch*, but the management was not going to allow Bulmers (excellent rail customers, would you believe) to get anything out of it this time. Instructions came from on high that, firstly, an anonymous locomotive should be provided and, second, that the journey was to be made at dead of night. In addition, although the locomotive had to be in steam to supply the cylinder oil atomisers for lubrication, the regulator handle would only be handed over on arrival. Although the publicity implicit in the fame of the locomotive was good for the firm, the real objective in having it was the haulage of the cider train out on the main line. *KGV* was steamed for VIP occasions at the works and in addition some local railway enthusiasts grouped themselves into the 6000 Locomotive Association. Under this banner they started to help with maintenance and organise open days, usually on bank holiday Mondays; in due time this led to the group's major involvement with the enterprise.

The arrival of a new Chairman, Sir Richard Marsh, at 222 Marylebone Road was the opportunity for one of his important customers to pay a call; at the meeting the question of a return to steam was discussed. Afterwards a copy of the planning department's paper on the subject was hurriedly sent for and soon enough a steam-hauled Cider Train Tour was agreed as an experiment, intended to find out whether any difficulties in the running of steam excursions were likely to arise.

On Saturday, 2 October, 1971, *King George V*, the locomotive that beat the ban, left Hereford for Severn Tunnel Junction, Swindon, Didcot and Oxford for Tyseley. The tender was refilled by fire brigades at Severn Tunnel Junction and Oxford. The train consisted of the five Bulmer's Pullmans for invited guests and five BR TSO's for fare-payers; it weighed 300 tons loaded, a featherweight load for a King. Enormous crowds were seen everywhere en route. Next morning and afternoon No 6000 paraded on the shuttle service at the Tyseley Open Day and on 4 October the train was worked from Birmingham (Moor Street) to Kensington (Olympia) on another excursion, where on the following day the locomotive was again on display. The next run was to Swindon, then via Bristol and the Severn Tunnel back to Hereford. The running was a counsel of perfection and no problems of any significance were encountered. Steam was back, if not for good then certainly for the time being.

Since then numerous successful and popular rail tours have been and still are being worked by No 6000, which in general has been confined to the Newport-Hereford-Shrewsbury-Chester route; in addition 57XX pannier tank No 7752, owned and maintained by the Worcester Railway Society serves for demonstrating steam inside the Bulmer's depot. *King George V* himself is a little too portly to work much outside GWR territory and, accordingly, was a noticeable absentee from both the Shildon 150 and Rocket 150 cavalcades. Indeed, in this connection, the engineering department, whose foresight allowed the Kings to exist in the first place, nearly finished the last of them off by encroaching on GWR clearances when lifting the track beneath an over-bridge on the Gloucester-Swindon line. No 6000 was on her way to Swindon by this rarely used (by steam) route when the top of the safety valve just caught the soffit of the arch; the valve was broken off, all the steam and much of the water in the boiler escaping instantly. The locomotive, of course, became a casualty, although very fortunately no lasting damage was done.

How much is owed to Bulmers and Peter Prior for causing to happen what all GWR enthusiasts now take for granted, the reader must judge for himself. But if ever anyone drinks a toast to our Cause's benefactors, they should at least have no doubts as to the beverage in which it is to be drunk.

12 Severn Valley Railway

Sir P. G. Wodehouse even at his most absurd frequently hit the nail on the head. Listen to him talking about the Great Western Railway in *Uncle Fred in the Springtime*, published in 1937 and still in print.

> The two-forty-five express – Paddington to Market Blandings, first stop Oxford – stood at its platform with that air of well-bred reserve that is characteristic of Paddington trains . . . for one living in Hampshire, there is something very soothing in the note of refined calm which Paddington strikes. At Waterloo, all is hustle and bustle and society tends to be mixed. Here a leisured peace prevails and you get only the best people – cultured men accustomed to mingling with basset hounds and women in tailored suits who look like horses.

Were one to set off from Paddington via Oxford on one of those 45-minute-past-the-hour expresses, with the intention of going to Shropshire avoiding the Black Country, the route, with a change at Worcester, takes you along the Severn Valley branch via Bridgnorth to Shrewsbury. And who knows but that a real Blandings Castle situated here might not have meant through trains from Paddington? The Earl of Emsworth himself would have been good material for the GWR Board; a locomotive – a small one such as the original Earl class named after himself might even have displaced his prize pig Empress of Blandings as his first enthusiasm. So it is particularly nice that this delightful Wodehousian line has become an immensely successful GWR preservation effort; indeed, many of the events connected with its recent rebirth have a considerable P. G. Wodehouse flavour about them including, of course, the happy ending.

The idea of a direct line for local as well as through north-south traffic avoiding the Black Country was floated as early as 1847, but it was not until 1853 that an Act was passed authorising the Severn Valley Railway Company to construct a line between Hartlebury, 12 miles north of Worcester, on the

Oxford, Worcester & Wolverhampton Railway (the old Worse & Worse) and Shrewsbury. Financial and engineering problems delayed completion and opening until 1 February, 1862, by which time the OW&W had become the West Midland Railway. From the opening the working was in the hands of the main-line company (West Midland until 1 August, 1863, then Great Western); the original SVR Co gave up its paper existence in 1872. In 1864, a branch from Bewdley through the Wyre Forest was opened, and in 1878 the connecting line between Kidderminster and Bewdley completed the drawing of the railway map of the area.

As so well depicted in the recent television series, *God's Wonderful Railway*, the line pursued a quiet existence over the years as an almost too typical GWR secondary line. In 1939 the train service consisted of five through first-and-third class trains from Worcester to Shrewsbury plus a number of one-class-only push-and-pull workings radiating from Bewdley. There were no expresses – all trains stopped at all stations – and no through carriages from Paddington or anywhere else, except for seasonal excursions.

In 1963 the line was closed to passenger traffic (except for the section from Kidderminster to Bewdley) as well as through freight trains and in 1965 the Severn Valley Railway Society was formed to preserve a section of the line. By 1966 the Society had got as far as agreeing with British Railways to buy the $4\frac{1}{2}$-mile section from Bridgnorth to Hampton Loade for £25,000; early in 1967 a 10 per cent deposit was paid. The first locomotive (GWR 0–6–0 No 3205) and carriages arrived at Bridgnorth soon after; an end-on connection with the main line system was maintained, since access for BR trains to the southern section of the line via Kidderminster was required in order to handle coal traffic from Arley colliery near Hampton Loade.

The new preserved line had a hard passage through the red tape jungle. The issue of planning consent had to go to appeal and afterwards the Light Railway Order process got into difficulties. This was because a new by-pass road was planned for Bridgnorth and the Ministry's road-builders again did not see why they should have to find the money for a new under-line bridge to carry a mere daisy-picking railway. The SVR negotiators, under the able leadership of Richard Dunn, were reluctantly prepared to accept the fact that when and if the by-pass was built, the railway would have to pay the cost of the road passing under the line. However, the Light Railways Act was designed to offer authority to railway builders either in perpetuity or not at all, so difficulties arose over drafting and agreeing suitable clauses in the Order to provide temporary authority. It was not until 20 May 1970 that the Society (now a Company Limited by Guarantee) received their authority to operate. Services began three days later; for some time they were only run at weekends.

Included in the deal with BR was an option to buy the rest of the Severn Valley line as far as Foley Park on the outskirts of Kidderminster. This additional 12 miles would make a run of $16\frac{1}{2}$ miles in all and would give the SVR a stake in the major tourist centre of Bewdley. It seemed a nice prospect for the distant future. A full weekday service was operated from 26 July until 11 August, for the operation of which many of the SVR's now famous corps of volunteers gave up their summer holidays. However, before the lively first season was over, BR announced that the remaining length of line was for sale, the coal trains and a residual service from Kidderminster to Bewdley having been withdrawn. So it happened that the infant company was faced with the prospect of having to run before it had learnt to walk.

Faced with the necessity to raise forthwith a sum in excess of £50,000, those in charge realised that the project was outside the range of a company limited by guarantee, an instrument which was intended for enterprises such as golf or tennis clubs. So it was accordingly considered necessary to call in capitalism; on the whole, members liked their small co-operative venture and the prospect of change led to some of the stormiest meetings in the history of railway preservation.

At the annual general meeting the following year the formation of a new company was announced which would take over the little co-op and its $4\frac{1}{2}$ miles of working railroad. That well-known moustachioed MP Sir Gerald Nabarro was to be chairman and the issued capital was to be £150,000. Many of those actually present did not fancy the man or his ideas, and so the debate was adjourned until more of the members could be canvassed. At a second meeting 670 members were present and three hours of lively debate followed the presentation of the directors' proposals. In the end the motion to go public was carried with only four votes against. 40,000 of the 150,000 £1 shares of the new company were reserved for the members of the guarantee company. It was decided later not to wind up the original company; instead, it became a holding company owning the 40,000 shares allocated to the original subscribers. The consequent public share issue of April 1972 was reasonably successful, £60,000 being raised. No dividends were to be paid but free tickets (below 100 shares, 2 third class; then up to 1000, 6 firsts; 1000 and above, gold pass) were some compensation.

Nevertheless, the working members were not happy with the new governing clique; they disapproved of several things Sir Gerald did. Finally, early in 1973, after he had dismissed Arthur Becker, the Operating Superintendent, the volunteers gave notice that they were not prepared to continue to give their services to the company as long as Sir Gerald remained chairman. In this way, preservation's first taste of the strike weapon achieved its object for shortly afterwards Viscount Garnock became the new chairman.

After all the shouting was over the SVR found itself in possession of what one could argue is the finest train set in Britain. Indisputably, the Victoria bridge over the River Severn, ½ mile south of Arley Station, an iron arch of 200ft span designed by Sir John Fowler of Forth Bridge fame, is the finest bridge on any preserved line. It should be added that when the company found the structure needed (eventually) £65,000 for repairs and strengthening, for a time I fancy the adjective used for it was a different one. The obligatory tunnel, half way between Bridgnorth and Eardington, like 'One Kiss Tunnel' on the Matheran Tramway near Bombay, India, is long enough to be excitingly dark, yet also sufficiently short not to be a liability. There is another and larger tunnel between Bewdley and Foley Park, but this is only used by special trains or on special occasions. The SVR came very close to having a junction, a railway feature that has so far eluded all preservers, GWR or otherwise. In fact, track was laid in for a short distance from Bewdley south along the abandoned roadbed towards Stourport, when the Sherlock Holmes film *The Seven Per Cent Solution* (of which the plot required a junction) was made on the SVR. But even though no longer normally a junction, Bewdley is the only preserved GWR station with more than two platform faces.

Before the new line could be used for public service, the usual bureaucratic rigmarole had to be endured. In the end BR obtained its Light Railway Order on 27 February, 1973, the SVR's Transfer Order following on 28 March, 1974. In the meantime substantial losses of £28,000 in 1973 and £16,000 in

1974, were being incurred, although they were in part due to the work being done in order to upgrade the line for axleloads up to 21 tons. This work was completed in September 1974. In Great Western terms the route colour was enhanced from blue to red, enabling such locomotives as Halls and Castles to be used; previously, Manors were the heaviest passenger engines allowed. 1974 was also the year in which the still-not-built by-pass bridge at Bridgnorth was placed in the 'firm' category, as part of the roads programme for that year.

Since then the story has been one of steady progress. In the five years from 1976 to 1980, the number of passengers carried has increased from 112,000 to over 180,000, while the number of members has gone up from 6,000 to over 10,000, the largest membership figure of any of the railway preservation societies. Particularly surprising was the big increase in 1980 compared with 1979, a time when many similar enterprises suffered reductions. It is arguable whether this is due to publicity resulting from the television series, *God's Wonderful Railway* or whether people in need of a steam fix now find a weekend in North Wales too expensive and so settle for a day out on the SVR.

Contributing to these results are the excellent scenery as well as the panache with which the SVR conducts its affairs. Excellent luncheons, afternoon teas and dinners are served in real GWR dining cars, as well as real beer in the Bridgnorth refreshment room, not to speak of the longest bar of any train in the world in GWR buffet car No 9631! It all helps to drum up a wide spectrum of custom. Other benefactors are the through BR special trains from faraway places in Britain via the Foley Park link; on one occasion in May 1980 two specials were handled on the same day plus the full advertised SVR train service.

To bring people on to the line, on certain days in 1979 and on a more regular basis in 1980, BR operated a public diesel-train link between Kidderminster and Bewdley. These included such great occasions as the annual Great Western weekend in the spring and the Enthusiasts weekend during autumn, which bring ferro-equinologists from far and wide; for the latter in 1980 12 locomotives were in steam, surely a record for any of the world's preservation enterprises and only eclipsed by combined operations such as jamborees on the scale of Rocket 150. The SVR, alone among the preserved GW operating railways, sends its locomotives and until recently its carriages out into the big world of BR, and quite exceptionally manages to make money in so doing. Furthermore, the company's excellent staff and equipment are in demand among less well-provided groups; outside work is now also a help in making the accounts healthy at year-end.

Among the benefits that financial success brings, quite soon in the future the SVR can look forward to having cover for its carriage fleet and so avoid frequent re-restoration. Already to hand are two turntables (one GWR from Whitchurch, Salop, but the other from far-away Fort William) which when installed at each end of the line will obviate the unattractive necessity for tender-first running. On the debit side the spectre of the by-pass bridge at Bridgnorth has not yet gone in spite of the 15-year delay. Meanwhile the company is displaying its confidence at being able to overcome this problem when it arises by extending the main platform there to take the longer trains needed for the increased traffic, which is so well deserved.

Even so, nothing described in this chapter or the next would be possible without the skills and devotion of the Severn Valley volunteers. These dedicated people turn out some 100 strong each weekend of the year, their only reward the fulfilment of their enthusiasm for GW railways and (often) GWR trains.

13 Severn Valley trains

Among the Severn Valley Railway's incredible 41-strong locomotive fleet – for the operation of a maximum three-train public service – are to be found 17 Great Western items. Of these all but one are of Swindon design. Only three of the designs preserved on the SVR are not to be found among Didcot's 19 GW locomotive exhibits, of which as many as six are of types not to be found on the SVR. Nevertheless, the composition of the fleet is remarkably representative, considering that it is intended to serve a working railway rather than a museum. Three 'threes' make up the backbone of the fleet; 57XX pannier tank 0–6–0s Nos 3612, 5764, 7719; 51XX 2–6–2T Nos 4141, 4150, 5164; 4–6–0s Nos 7802 *Bradley Manor*, 7812 *Erlestoke Manor*, and 7819 *Hinton Manor*. The largest engines on the line are 4–6–0s Nos 4930 *Hagley Hall*, 6960 *Raveningham Hall* and 28XX 2–8–0 No 2857, while two 'singletons' are 45XX 2–6–2T No 4566 and 43XX 2–6–0 No 9303.

The three exhibits of types or classes not to be seen elsewhere are first, a Hudswell-Clarke 0–6–0 saddle tank shunting locomotive which came into GWR possession (as No 813) via the Port Talbot Railway, for which she was built as No 26 in 1901. For the second, the starting point is the legendary Dean Goods 0–6–0 design mentioned several times in these pages; in 1930, Swindon produced the 2251 class 0–6–0, a modernised version of the Dean Goods, with taper boiler and side-window cab. A further batch was built after the war and the example preserved on the SVR (No 3205) was one of these. She was the first locomotive to arrive on the line, back in 1965. The third and last fresh example of GW preservation goes back to a remark made at the head of Chapter 5 in that the GWR's remarkable standardisation policy bulged just a little towards the end. On the SVR can be found one of the bulges. For some reason, not clear – maybe it was just boredom or perhaps another Marylebone-Road-tease – the WR chief mechanical engineer's department in 1949 built a few shunting locomotives to a radically changed design, in an attempt to improve on what was one of the best-ever, most highly-developed and longest-standardised designs ever produced for this purpose, the 57XX class. I suppose one could argue that little 1501 and her nine sisters, built in 1949, are not GW-built locomotives, but even so she is aesthetically very pleasing and no doubt her owners had this in mind when they made the acquisition.

Not a new type but different in her way is 43XX 2–6–0 No 9303, one of a batch built in 1930, much later than the rest of the class, most of which dated from Churchward days, ie before 1922. The main difference is the Collett cab with side windows. This neat little engine is owned by the Great Western (SVR) Association, not the SVR Co itself, which brings me to another point. One thing new among the large preserved fleets so far reviewed is that the management of the SVR always allowed and indeed encouraged independent ownership, relying on common purpose and dedication to produce the discipline needed for running a commercial operation. In fact the only GWR locomotive owned by the SVR Co directly is No 4930 *Hagley Hall*. Howwell the arrangement works is shown by the amazingly high proportion – over 50 per cent – of the Great Western fleet on the SVR which is currently operable. Such a figure is unmatched elsewhere among the preserved lines. The runners (of July 1980) were Nos 2857, 3205, 4566, 4930, 6960, 5164, 7812, and 7819. With restoration well under way are 1501, 4141, 7714, while 813, 4150 and 9303 are longer-term candidates for this process. Nos 3612 and 7802 are on the property as a source of spare parts rather than with any intention of being put to rights. Among the runners, No 3205 is interesting in that she bore the brunt of operation having been the first to arrive on the line in 1965. She handled the first passenger train in 1970, but had to be laid aside for overhaul and re-restoration in 1973. This process took seven years but was completed just in time for an equally distinguished debut the second time round, by carrying the SVR flag during the Rocket 150 cavalcade at Rainhill.

Out of 58 passenger train vehicles on the Severn Valley Railway, 27 or nearly half are of both Great Western and Swindon origin. All have been acquired for use rather than ornament, but those in traffic have been beautifully restored, so making the best of both worlds. SVR carriage restoration stands out even among the very high standards achieved on lines and depots elsewhere.

All the common twentieth century design families are represented so that in this respect there is nothing on the SVR that cannot be found at Didcot. However, the line does offer one fresh thing – GWR refreshment vehicles. A diner-pair dating from the bow-end era, consisting of kitchen-first No 9615 and restaurant-third saloon No 9625, offers meal service, while buffet No 9631 (of the 1934–35 economy carriage family) on loan from the National Collection can handle large demands for liquid refreshment from its 40-elbow bar running the full length of the vehicle. Regular Luncheon and Dining Car Expresses are something way above anything provided on the Severn Valley line in the old days. Observation car trains can be provided too, using engineer's inspection saloon No 80969 of 1948 which like most inspection vehicles has end windows.

Apart from 80969, the whole fleet is of the corridor type and the table on page 89 indicates how it is spread among the various functions and design families. The asterisks indicate vehicles not yet restored for use.

One might wonder what use the sleeping cars serve on an 18-mile railway until one realises that they provide cheap and comfortable accommodation for the volunteers upon whom the SVR relies so wholly for its continuance.

Severn Valley GWR Dining Car trains known as the Severn Valley Limited have also run long distances out on British Railways, both on main-line steam specials and on charter trains with BR motive power. When this occurs regular services over the SVR itself can be maintained by sets of stock from other companies. So far as possible SVR trains consist of stock from one former owner only, that is all GWR or all LMS, the other company represented on the SVR.

The fact that freight is not handled by the Severn Valley does not prevent it having a 17-strong GW wagon fleet partly for interest and partly for service use. Noted are a SIPHON G milk van, a MACAW B bogie bolster, four FRUIT D vans, a Banana van, a MOGO motor car van, a MICA B refrigerated van, four other vans, a LORIOT machinery wagon, one china clay wagon and a standard wagon. Two TOAD brake vans complete the set, except for a passenger fruit van and a milk train brake van equipped with brake gear, couplings and buffers suitable for running in passenger trains.

Above: Didcot line-up of National Railway Museum items on 5 October 1980. Left to right is the *Rocket* replica, 0-4-0WT No 5 *Shannon*, SR 4-6-2 *Winston Churchill* and Class 9F 2-10-0 No 92220 *Evening Star*. *Richard Brown*

Below: Coach preservation: 1930s excursion third No 1289 as restored by the Didcot team seen in 1979. *Michael Baker*

Great Western preserved locomotive meets Great Western preserved coaches when Dart Valley Railway 2-8-0T No 5239, now named *Goliath*, heads up the Torbay & Dartmouth line from Kingswear with the returning Torbay Limited train formed of the Great Western Society's preserved coaches on 12 May 1979. *Mark Wilkins*

Carriage Type	57ft Toplight 1908–1923	57ft Bow-end 1923–1933	60ft Economy 1934–1935	61ft Yellow Disc 1938–1948	65ft Post-War 1948–1955
Third	2426* 3930*			1086 1087 1116 1146	829 2119
Composite		6045*		7284	
Brake Third			5883		
Brake Composite			6912* 6913	6562	
Sleeping Car First					9082* 9084* 9085*
Full brake	1145*			98*	
Saloon	9055* 9369	9103*		80969	
Dining Car First Third		9615* 9627			
Buffet Car			9631		
Auto Coach		178			

89

Another 15 GWR wagons are included in the service fleet, with wagons for rail (GANE A), sleepers and ballast (two), nine vans from breakdown trains (five riding, four tool) plus a shunters truck and a signal department wagon; it is a useful collection, which serves the railway well in dealing with its formidable engineering problems.

14 West Somerset and other GWR lines

We have seen more than once that the Great Western Railway was a feudal organisation where everyone and everything knew their place. In respect of its branches, two pointers to social status were, one, whether first-class accommodation was provided and, two, whether through carriages ran from Paddington. Of those lines already dealt with none have both these U-train attributes except the Torbay line of the DVR which, with once two named daily Luncheon and Tea Car expresses (the Torbay Limited and the Devonian), really belongs up above among the main-line aristocracy. So perhaps it could be said that coverage from a social status point of view was not quite complete.

To fill this gap, if gap it is, the Minehead branch is amply qualified and more. The through coach from Paddington was in the old days slipped at Taunton from the Cornish Riviera Limited, no less, and naturally the slip coach became two or more dining car trains on summer Saturdays. It was also a rather superior line in that the passing loops were laid out for speeds of 40mph instead of 15. Accordingly (and, with the Barnstaple branch, unique on the GWR) automatic token exchange was provided with apparatus at the lineside and on the fleet of eight 45XX class 2–6–2Ts which worked the branch. Lineage was also impeccable, the line having been broad gauge for the first years of its existence.

The original West Somerset Railway was promoted under the chairmanship of someone called Sir Peregrine Acland and received authorisation by Parliament in 1857 for a broad gauge line from Norton Fitzwarren, three miles south-west of Taunton, to Watchet. It was opened for passengers on 31 March, 1862 and (rather strangely) five months *later* for freight. From the first the line was worked by the Bristol & Exeter Railway and then the GWR from 1876 when the latter absorbed the B&E, but the West Somerset company as such pursued an independent

91

existence until absorbed into the GWR in 1922. The extension to Minehead had a similar history; it was opened in July 1874 and absorbed into the GWR in 1897. Conversion of gauge from broad to standard took place in 1882; 500 men attacked the line with such vigour at daybreak on Sunday 29 October that a narrow gauge inspection special was able to reach Minehead soon after mid-day. Minehead grew in popularity as a resort during the 1920s to an extent sufficient for the branch and its approaches to receive considerable attention during the big government-assisted GWR new works schemes of the 1930s. The main line between Taunton and Norton Fitzwarren was quadrupled, Norton Fitzwarren to Bishops Lydeard was doubled, as was the last section of line from Dunster to Minehead. In order to even out the spacing of the passing places, essential in order to run the intensive summer Saturday train service, new lonely crossing loops were provided at Leigh Bridge between Crowcombe and Stogumber and at Kentsford, between Watchet and Washford. The existing station loops at Crowcombe and Blue Anchor were lengthened and improved.

Closure took place in 1971 against much local opposition, but the area was evidently not marginal enough politically (compared with other much less appropriate places) for the line to be put on Westminster's list for retention. So the local authority decided to go it alone and support on a very large scale the attempt by an amateur group to re-open the line. The line and trackwork was bought by the Somerset County Council for £245,000 and the new company loaned £60,000 at a low rate of interest – just like that. After some opposition and an adjourned inquiry, the Light Railway Order was granted to BR on 18 November 1974; the transfer order to the new West Somerset Railway Company came on 1 September 1975. As a result public train services over the $3\frac{1}{2}$ miles between Minehead and Watchet were able to begin on 28 March, 1976. It was agreed that an annual rent of £14,000 was payable to the SCC to be reduced to £4,000 if the railway company operated daily commuter services. At a later stage the company received a grant of a further £72,000 under the Job Creation Scheme.

One might ask how much the Great Western enthusiast-taxpayer got for an outlay of nearly £400,000 of public money, the equivalent of over a million in today's pounds. The answer, I'm afraid, is very little; but satisfying GWR enthusiasts was not the object of the enterprise. At the time of writing only one GW locomotive has been used on the line – 64XX pannier tank No 6412, purchased from the Dart Valley Railway. Other than two 45XX carcases from Barry (Nos 4561 and 5542) not yet restored, the motive power is composed mainly of industrial shunters. One might, of course, stretch a point and say that the ex-London, Brighton & South Coast Railway Terrier 0–6–0T at Minehead could stand in for two examples of these famous locomotives which came into GWR possession in 1940. This was the result of the GWR purchase of the assets of the defunct Weston, Clevedon & Portishead Railway, the line with the famous initials that invited one to visit the WC&P!

So far no passengers have been carried in GWR carriages on the WSR, although three toplight camping coaches are on the property. Currently year-round daily-except-Sunday diesel services are operated using ex-BR multiple-unit power cars or a Hymek diesel-hydraulic locomotive. Steam operations are confined to summer Sundays and Wednesdays and have achieved a certain fame through the television series Flockton Flyer, which was filmed on the line and starred No 6412. The WSR is famous for having pioneered a residential holiday course in steam locomotive maintenance, cleaning, firing and driving. Alas it has not yet been possible for WSR trains to run beyond Bishops Lydeard to Norton Fitzwarren and Taunton because of objections by the National Union of Railwaymen who staff the buses, and a bus link has to be used. If and when all the line comes in use throughout, the WSR at $19\frac{3}{4}$ miles will be the longest preserved railway in the country.

The WSR will not, however, be the longest preserved ex-GWR line in the country; three of the restored ex-GWR canals exceed it in length by a comfortable margin. The Oxford, Worcester & Wolverhampton Railway bought the Stratford Canal in 1857; hence it became GWR property in 1863, remaining so until handed over to the British Waterways Board after nationalisation. The canal is $25\frac{1}{2}$ miles long and runs from Kings Norton Junction with the Worcester & Birmingham Canal to the River Avon at Stratford, a distance of $25\frac{1}{2}$ miles with two iron aquaducts, a 352yd tunnel and 56 narrow gauge locks. The section south of Lapworth, closed in 1958, was the subject of an historic and massive volunteer restoration effort between 1960 and 1964.

The Brecon & Abergavenny Canal was another of the GWR's less appreciated possessions. It came into GWR ownership in

1880 as one of the Monmouthshire Railway & Canal Company's assets, at which time commercial traffic upon it had already ceased. Although as much as 33 miles long, there are only six locks. The engineering works are heavy and include a 375yd tunnel, as well as deep rock cuttings and substantial embankments. It was re-opened to recreational navigation in 1970, after a joint restoration scheme by the BWB and the Monmouthshire County Council. Scenically the canal is second to none, says Bryan Marsh in the *Good Boat Guide* (Penguin Books, 1980).

Greatest of all the Great Western Canals was the 60-mile Kennet & Avon Canal which effectively connected the Thames at Reading via the Kennet Navigation to the Avon at Bath. The waterway came into the GWR's possession in 1857 and is currently the object of a massive restoration effort. Engineering works include a long summit tunnel at Savernake, steam pumping stations with working beam engines at Claverdon, near Bath, and at Crofton, near Savernake, as well as the famous staircase of 29 contiguous locks at Devizes. As a junior assistant in the Paddington Divisional Engineer's office during 1947, the writer found himself for two weeks (when someone was on holiday) not only as Canal Engineer but also Traffic Superintendent and Commercial Manager of this great artery of commerce. There was even traffic in the form of a small motor yacht whose skipper had approval to work the locks on his own. As an illustration of the state of affairs on the canal, following a complaint from the Canal Inspector that this person had not 'racked up the sluices' properly, a letter was written to him. The reply was most aggrieved in tone and it turned out that in K&A parlance 'racking up the sluices' meant cutting sods of turf from the banks and using them to stop up the cascading leaks which inevitably appeared after a sluice-gate had been operated. Incidentally, during the same year a barge-load of Hovis flour was experimentally worked from Bristol to London; this was the only commercial movement within the memory of those then connected with the canal. Experience was such that it was not repeated.

Returning to activities for which the GWR is better known, two better-than-minor branches in Wales are also in process of having nominal sections revived. The term 'revived' rather than 'preserved' is used advisedly because in both cases new track is having to be laid on an abandoned road-bed. The Ruabon to

Barmouth Junction line would in the 1930s have been an even better case for modernisation than Taunton to Minehead; on the other hand its length of 53 miles made it an even worse case for preservation. The pleasant station in the centre of the world-famous town of Llangollen, as well as the scenic course of the railway westwards, attracted a group of enthusiasts known as the Flint & Deeside Railway Society. Progress with the project has meant a change of name to the Llangollen Railway Society Ltd. The plan is eventually to open five miles of line as far as the exceptionally beautifully sited station at Glyndyfrdwy. The first GWR locomotive (57XX pannier tank No 7754) has recently arrived on site and track-laying has started. There is an ex-GWR brake third coach of 1938, No 5539.

The Gwili Valley Railway is similarly attempting to put back into use a short length of a line that once was intended to make Milford Haven in Pembrokeshire the port for Manchester by means of a railway crossing the mountains of Mid-Wales. Not surprisingly very little of the Manchester & Milford Railway was actually built, and this eventually became part of the GWR Carmarthen to Aberystwyth line. The revival covers $1\frac{1}{4}$ miles from Bronwydd Arms to Cwmdyfran and it is noted that the Gwili Railway Company's address is Great Western Chambers, Angel Street (where else?), Neath. GWR rolling stock on site comprises yet-to-be-restored Manor class 4–6–0 *Dinmore Manor* and the body only of ex-Taff Vale Railway brake third of 1891, GWR No 3846.

At Caerphilly, Mid-Glamorgan, there is the Harold Wilson Industrial Estate, once better known as the Rhymney Railway (and later the GWR) locomotive works. Half a mile of track is available for demonstration steamings of items either on loan to or owned by the National Museum of Wales. The principal GWR exhibit is unique and is, in addition, the archetypal South Wales locomotive. This is ex-Taff Vale Railway class O1 0–6–2T No 28 (GWR No 450) built by the TVR's own works at Cardiff in 1897. It was presented to the NMOW by the National Coal Board, which made the last use of the locomotive. It is one of the very few Welsh-built standard gauge locomotives and the only one preserved.

Just across the border into England but not far away is another scheme, the long-standing ambition of the Dean Forest Railway Preservation Society. This group for many years has been collecting GWR material at what became a working museum at Norchard, Gloucestershire, as will be described later. The patience displayed by the Society has finally paid off and negotiations have begun for this by now fairly experienced organisation to take over the 3½-mile Lydney to Parkend line. If all goes as planned, the scheme will be very attractive and practical, with a good deal of Great Western action and a terminus in the Forest of Dean National Forest Park.

Further out of Wales into Somerset, England and also far advanced is a 1¼ mile section of the line running from Witham to Yatton. This is known as the East Somerset Railway and is based on the working museum at Cranmore station, the project of artist David Shepherd. No Great Western action is envisaged, however, not even the possibility of a feasting one's eyes on a humble wagon of that company. Down in the deeper South West a group is aiming to put tracks back on the abandoned bed of the line up the Plym Valley which once formed the GWR route from Plymouth to Tavistock and Launceston. Already a 41XX 2-6-2T and Southern West Country 4-6-2, both requiring restoration, have been acquired.

Even more problematical as a prospect for running GWR trains is the proposal of an optimistic group known as the Swindon & Cricklade Railway Society to restore from scratch a section of the old Midland & South Western Junction Railway in the Swindon area. The same applies to the Gloucestershire & Warwickshire Railway Company (note the initials) which has similar aspirations regarding a surviving section of the Cheltenham and Honeybourne line.

15 Museums in GW territory

Right in the epicentre of Great Western territory, in the town of Swindon, is an excellent museum situated in what was an old chapel building very close to the railway station. While you might at first take away marks because its exhibits are wholly static, you must then give them all back again because four out of five full-size locomotive exhibits there are of important classes, examples of which cannot be found elsewhere.

The oldest, the only significant Great Western survivor from the Victorian age, is one of the legendary Dean Goods 0–6–0s. All GWR enthusiasts rejoiced when one of them was tested against a BR standard class 2 2–6–0 of similar power (and 65 years her junior) and the old lady proved to be far superior both in economy and haulage ability. Other Dean Goods have travelled in most countries in Europe and in 1946 some even went further afield.

City of Truro was the heroine of that episode already mentioned when she was driven all-out to 'do the ton' down Wellington Incline. This 4–4–0 represents as the sole example, a whole range of Edwardian GWR steam power; her close relatives, the Atbaras, the Flowers and the Bulldogs have all gone to their long home.

The Star class was a milestone in GWR locomotive history; they were the prototypes of most subsequent GWR express locomotives, the Knights, the Abbeys, the Castles and both lots of Kings. Aside from a few rebels such as the writer, who believe that their qualities existed in spite of, rather than because of, the complexities of their mechanical layout, most GWR enthusiasts stand with some awe looking up at the lovely lineaments of 4–6–0 *Lode Star*.

9400 is an example of what could be regarded as either one of the pannier tank classes with a taper boiler or a 22XX 0–6–0 converted to a pannier tank. This class was the last GWR design to be constructed, examples appearing as late as 1956; some of

97

the later ones had extraordinarily short lives.

Lastly, there is a full-size replica, incorporating a few parts of the original, of the very first locomotive to run on the GWR, Robert Stephenson & Co's immortal broad gauge *North Star*. This is the nearest it is possible to get to the locomotives which hauled the trains on Brunel's famous broad gauge railways. Unlike her prototype, the replica is at least a Swindon engine!

The smaller exhibits at Swindon are also exceedingly fine and, having enjoyed them, one can return to Paddington in an afternoon train which at last cuts (by two minutes) the 65min public timing for that journey, achieved in 1933. It was not until 45 years later that British Rail offered anything faster!

Having said such unkind things twice already about the standard Great Western four-cylinder layout, it seems a little odd to the writer that in order to represent the whole of British latter-day steam by one example, the Science Museum in London chose No 4073 *Caerphilly Castle*. There is another way of looking at it, of course; able people need a challenge and as long as it is made to seem worthwhile, the harder the job, the more satisfying it is. Now the Castles, as we have seen, were wonderful performers – that 65min timing from Swindon to Paddington, a world record for many years, was entrusted to them – and handling just for a few minutes different locomotive bits and pieces would convince anyone that, as regards workmanship, the rest of the world was nowhere in comparison with Swindon. The fact that they were almost but not quite impossible to maintain merely meant that they got good maintenance. Anyway, as she is now, restored in all her glory, No 4073 is indeed a sight worth seeing.

Without trespassing too far into the next chapter, which concerns pastures new for GWR wheels, we note 19 places so far not mentioned where something Great Western can be found. The twentieth is that ex-GWR station called Cranmore (part of the East Somerset Railway referred to in Chapter 14) near Shepton Mallet in Somerset, which has been converted into an elegant museum stuffed with remarkable full-size railway exhibits, but is notable in that *none* of them, not even an open wagon or shunters truck, are Great Western!

Six only among the others offer Swindon locomotives, none of them of fresh classes, but restored and put together they would make a nice broad-based collection. There is even another King at Quainton Road depot, near Aylesbury; this is No 6024, *King*

Edward I, a hulk from Barry at present undergoing the lengthy process of being raised from the dead. Similarly, there is the only 94XX 0-6-0T intended not to be stuffed and mounted, No 9466. The Quainton Railway Society Ltd also has another standard pannier tank, No 7715, ex-London Transport No L99. A full brake built in 1938 is also present.

That Dean Forest Railway Society at Norchard, Gloucestershire, has 45XX and 41XX 2-6-2Ts and a 57XX 0-6-0PT (Nos 5541, 5521, 5523, 4121 and 9681) as well as a 1938 brake third, an auto-coach and some freight stock. Another 57XX pannier tank has been restored by the 9462 Preservation Group at the National Coal Board workshops at Maesteg in South Wales. At Tiverton Museum, Devon, one of the 14XX class that worked the branches which used to run in three directions from the town (to Exeter, to Tiverton Junction and to Dulverton) is on display there. Further north, in the Welsh border country, is 56XX 0-6-2T No 5619 on display in Telford New Town and, more excitingly, No 7822 *Foxcote Manor* under restoration by the Foxcote Manor Society at Oswestry. The London area has the Great Western Group, at Bridge Road, Southall, Middlesex with 41XX 2-6-2T No 4110, at present in the early stages of restoration after recovery from the Barry scrapyard. Other items are expected.

Of three rather small and untypical locomotives from the GWR's Welsh constituents, it is odd that, in spite of Wales being so strong in the preservation of old railways, two of them are preserved outside the Principality. Ex-Cardiff Railway 0-4-0 saddle tank No 1338 is on display at the Somerset Railway Museum at Uphill, Bleadon, south of Bristol; she was built by Kitsons of Leeds in 1898. Another 0-4-0T (GWR No 921) which shunted the Swansea Docks under the banner of the firm of Powlesland & Mason, before it was taken over by the GWR, has somehow found its way to the Municipal Museum in Leicester. Leicester, of course, was GWR territory in the sense that Great Western locomotives ran in and out of the city on Great Central metals, but the types used did not include tiny dock shunters from West Wales!

Really in West Wales and situated in the Pembrokeshire County Museum, Scolton House, near Haverfordwest is the 0-6-0 saddle tank *Margaret* (GWR No 1378) supplied new for the infant North Pembroke & Fishguard Railway in 1878.

Of locations that offer coaches, the most interesting is the sole survivor of those two fabulous Centenary train sets built specially for the Cornish Riviera Limited in 1935. Diner 9635 is at the Dowty Railway Preservation Society near Ashchurch, Gloucestershire, in company with special clerestory saloon No 9044 (of 1881), a 3-ton hand crane and a Coral A glass-carrying wagon.

The only coach to survive from the South Wales constituent companies is Taff Vale brake-third No 203 of 1912 being restored at a site near Bath, while the Cornish Steam Locomotive Preservation Society has a near-contemporary toplight third (No 2434) on its site at Bugle near St Austell. The official Bristol Industrial Museum has some sections of old broad gauge carriage bodies and an old six-wheeled tri-composite (No 820 of 1886); there is also a goods brake and a Mogo motor car van. A stone ballast wagon, another goods brake and a 6-ton hand crane are the only GWR exhibits among a numerous collection of rolling stock being restored by the Caerphilly Railway Society at its site on the Harold Wilson Industrial Estate.

An extreme rarity in the world is a private garden railway of full-size (4ft 8½in) gauge. One exists at the home of Bill McAlpine at Fawley near Henley-on-Thames; contractors' type locomotives discarded by the family firm form the motive power fleet, but a GWR goods brake van is used as a riding van and observation car. The line includes 1 in 14 gradients!

In the proposal stage is a museum at Treviscoe, Cornwall, based on the Brunel goods shed from Lostwithiel re-erected. Two GWR locomotives are set aside for this Cornwall Locomotive Group from among those lying as scrap at Barry, South Wales.

This particular scrapyard has now become an unlikely place of pilgrimage for steam lovers. Over 50 Swindon locomotives are presently rusting away in the soft sea air in the now famous premises of Woodham Bros, scrap dealers. All GWR enthusiasts owe a great deal to the Woodhams, who bought hundreds of locomotives from British Rail during the Götterdammerung of steam in the 1960s; 88 of these were of Great Western origin. Most of the copper, brass and bronze fittings were then removed and sold, thus paying for the locomotives. The remains were left for the price of scrap-iron and steel to rise to a level which would pay for the cost of cutting the engines up.

One of the conditions of the contract of sale with BR was that the locomotives should not be re-sold except as scrap. At first this

Class	Type	No.	Name	Date Built	Possible Destination
28XX	2–8–0	2807		1903	Churchward Consolidation Fund
		2885		1938	GWR Preservation Group, Southall
		3862		1942	Cornwall Locomotive Group
42XX	2–8–0T	4247		1916	Peak Park Railway, Buxton
		4270		1920	GWR Steam Preservation Group, Swansea
Hall	4–6–0	4979	Wootton Hall	1930	Quainton Railway Society
		5967	Bickmarsh Hall	1935	Cornwall Locomotive Group
56XX	0–6–2T	5668		1926	Peak Park Railway, Buxton
		6634		1928	GWR Preservation Group; Southall
		6695		1928	GWR Steam Preservation Group, Swansea
King	4–6–0	6023	King Edward II	1930	6023 Group
72XX	2–8–2T	7200		1934	Quainton Railway Society

101

condition was rigidly enforced, but the thin end of what became eventually a very large wedge was inserted when the Great Western Society wanted to add to their collection a class 43XX 2–6–0 as has been related in Chapter 4. Since then more than 30 GWR locomotives (all Swindon-designed and most Swindon-built) have left Barry; approximately half have been successfully restored and no doubt most of the others will follow.

More of these grisly exhibits have been ear-marked for preservation by being reserved for various restoration groups. Some will have been taken away by the time this book is read; the aspiring owners of some of the others will fail to raise the money needed for purchase and movement. The list of potential rescues is shown on p. 101.

The 38 ex-GWR hulks that remain unclaimed at Barry, have been so well picked over by people in search of spare parts that it is hardly practicable to regard them as objects of restoration. Of course, the very possibility of doing anything to these now pathetic objects is just what attracts people who enjoy a challenge. For the record, their details are as follows:

2–8–0	28XX	2859/61/73/4, 3802/3/14/45/50/55/62
2–6–2T	51XX	4115/56, 5199
2–8–0T	42XX	4248/53/77, 5227
0–6–0T	57XX	4612/9629/9682
4–6–0	Hall	4936 *Kinlet Hall*, 4953 *Pitchford Hall*, 5972 *Olton Hall*, 6984 *Owsden Hall*, 7903 *Foremarke Hall*, 7927 *Willington Hall*
2–6–2T	45XX	5526/32/38/39/52/53
0–6–2T	56XX	6686
2–8–2T	72XX	7229
4–6–0		7802 *Bradley Manor*, 7821 *Ditcheat Manor*, 7828 *Odney Manor*

16 Great Western in pastures new

Preserved Great Western wheels are especially far-flung, perhaps more so than others. One reason for this is simply that they were available; the Woodham Brothers' treasure trove in South Wales, for quite simple geographical reasons, contained more GWR material than any others. There was also the steam fleet of London Transport which lasted several years longer than BR and was wholly ex-GWR at the end. The other reason is that the brassy green beauty of GWR locomotives and the elegance of the high gloss chocolate-and-cream finish of the carriages are a proper challenge to preservers faced with a rusty hulk from Barry or a hen house from Somerset. Of 17 places in question, eight have Swindon locomotives, two have no locomotives but carriages, while the rest have only wagons.

The National Railway Museum at York is arguably the finest in the world, but not, it must be added, in relation to the Great Western Railway, towards which it nicely levels (as regards material on display) with the Outback of Western Australia. There is only one Swindon product among the 30-odd locomotives on display, but that is the one that says it all. This is 28XX 2–8–0 No 2818 of 1905, which put a new dimension into trunk freight haulage when the class appeared in 1903. Many parts were standard with GWR 4–6–0s and nothing better than a 28 was produced for freight haulage in Britain for nearly 50 years. 2818 is currently one of several 28s and 38s to be restored. Welshpool & Llanfair 2ft 6in gauge 0–6–0T *The Earl*, once owned by the GWR, is also to be seen but, otherwise, GWR rolling stock on display at the NRM is trivial.

The NRM has a great deal of material put aside which is not on public exhibition. In some cases this is because the item concerned is not yet restored, but in general the reason is that, in spite of the museum's enormous size, there just is not enough space for everything to be displayed. Several interesting GWR items are thus temporarily hidden away including one of the very

103

early path-finding GWR diesel railcars. No 4 was built by AEC bus builders of Southall, Middlesex as long ago as 1934. While others of the batch were intended for light-weight local services, this one (No 4) was for the fast Birmingham-Gloucester-Cardiff Inter-City operation; it even included a buffet counter in its accommodation. It was successful to the point that the traffic generated soon led to replacement by a locomotive-hauled train.

Three GWR carriages were acquired when the hush-hush emergency control trains were disbanded recently. Bow-ended third-class dining saloons Nos 9653 and 9654 are relics of the triplet diners of the articulated express trains built in 1925. The stock was rebuilt as non-articulated in the 1930s and these two cars are the only known survivors. End-kitchen composite dining car No 9605 was one of a batch of ten single-unit cars built in 1930. When the GWR designed composite diners (instead of classless vehicles) it was usual for the kitchen to be placed in the centre; this batch of vehicles was one of the exceptions. Perhaps this points at a fundamental problem in museum-keeping. Contemporary experts are interested in the unusual while posterity will want to see the norm. An even more vivid illustration of this point is the set of signals set very conspicuously outside the walls at the approach to the museum. This particular group of signals from Oxford was unique and the GW signal department's idea of how they would make upper-quadrant semaphore signals if they ever had to; but both before and after, in spite of great pressure to standardise with the rest of BR virtually all GW and Western Region semaphores are of the lower-quadrant pattern.

A way in which the NRM makes its surplus stock available for the public to see is by lending items out to other museums. A famous locomotive lent out in this way is ex-Great Central 2–8–0 No 102 of 1911, now at the Dinting Steam Centre near Manchester. This example of a famous design was never in GWR possession, but as many as 100 others were (though not all at one time, I think), all bought as surplus stock from the Ministry of Munitions after the first world war. Others came on loan. In the end 50 of the RODs, as they were called, survived, well liked in spite of their foreign origin, and gave good service on the GWR for about 30 years. Relevant to this but not strictly in place here one notes the similar case of one of the war-babies of the second world war, LMS class 8F 2–8–0 No 8431, now preserved on the Keighley & Worth Valley Line. This locomotive was built by the

Above: Dart Valley Railway 0-4-2T No 1420 leaves Staverton for Buck-fastleigh with a train of former Great Western coaches. *C. H. S. Owen*
Below: One of the Dart Valley Railway's two 45XX 2-6-2Ts, No 4588, seen here at Paignton. *Courtesy Dart Valley Railway*

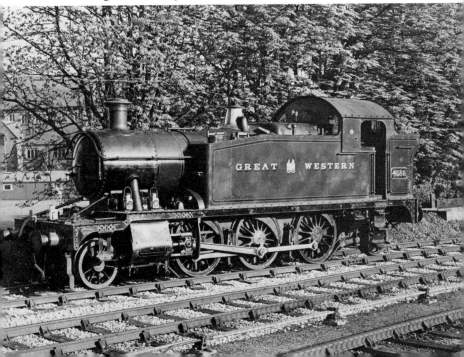

Above: The only line to retain Great Western locomotives and coaches exactly as in Great Western days, though in new colours, is the narrow gauge Vale of Rheidol line where 2-6-2T No 8 *Llywelyn* is seen leaving the old VoR station at Aberystwyth. *T. Wright*

Below: Tyseley: No 4983 *Albert Hall* is seen in the erecting shop under restoration. *P. B. Whitehouse*

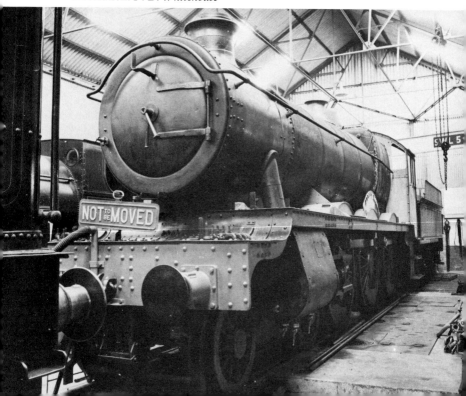

GWR at Swindon in 1944 to the LMS design and must have been momentarily in the GWR's possession before it was paid for!

The Keighley & Worth Valley Railway does however have two quite genuine GWR locomotives. 57XX pannier tank No 5775 of 1929 masquerades in crimson-lake as London Transport No L89, her last assignment before preservation. She starred (in strange buff-coloured garb) in the film *The Railway Children*. The KWVR also has on the property an ex-Taff Vale O2 class 0–6–2T, No 85, (GWR No 426) built by Neilson, Reid & Co. of Glasgow in 1899.

Scattered around the North are various other GWR tank locomotives. There are 56XX 0–6–2Ts both on the North Yorkshire Moors Railway and at Steamtown Museum, Carnforth. At Steamport (Southport) there is a 61XX 2–6–2T. The Peak Park Railway at Buxton, Derbyshire, has a 42XX 2–8–0T and another 56XX 0–6–2T reserved for them at Barry; but of all the material preserved or to be preserved outside Great Western territory, none is more significant than a locomotive on the Bluebell Railway, No 3217, *Earl of Berkeley*, one of the actual locomotives that Chief Mechanical Engineer Charles B. Collett had named after titled gentlemen, as described in Chapter 4. The name was allocated to, rather than actually carried by, No 3217 when she was completed in March 1938. The present nameplates were fitted on preservation.

The class has a rather curious and informal origin; K. J. Cook describes in his 'horse's mouth' account of GWR locomotive building, *Swindon Steam* (Ian Allan, 1965) how, as Works Manager he was in the erecting shop one day in 1930. Alongside Bulldog No 3365 (at one time named *Charles Grey Mott*) was Duke No 3264 *Tre Pol and Pen*; it suddenly struck him that a Duke boiler on a Bulldog chassis would make a locomotive far more suitable for the steeply-graded but lightly-constructed main line of the old Cambrian Railways than anything else then available. He then and there gave instructions for the change to be made. Oswestry was delighted with the 'Super-Duke', and between 1936 and 1939 production batches of these conversions totalled 29 locomotives. Our survivor, No 3217, was converted from the chassis of No 3425 and (on paper anyway) Duke No 3258 *The Lizard*.

No 3217 is the most important GWR exhibit to be found on other than Great Western territory and represents not only her own class, but also the Duke class, the Badmintons and, indeed, all the 4–4–0 passenger locomotives designed by Dean. This was in spite of being put together 36 years after that gentleman retired. For her preservation we are indebted to Mr. T. R. Gomm of Birmingham, whose firm is well known for those famous locomotive badges sold by every railway preservation establishment. She went to the Bluebell Railway soon after purchase in 1960, really because there was then no other choice; since this line was soon to be isolated from the rest of the railway system, it was never thought possible to make a move. As BR No 9017, this last survivor of the Dukedogs was also the last double-framed locomotive, complete with outside cranks, to run in Britain other than as a museum piece. She was also the first GWR locomotive to be bought for preservation, even before 1466 or 4555.

Just outside the normal range of operation of GWR locomotives is the new Great Central Railway Co. at Loughborough, just north of Leicester. Here one can find yet another Hall class 4–6–0 No 6990 *Witherslack Hall*, as well as 2–8–0T No 5227. Similarly, just outside GWR locomotive-range is 0–6–2T No 6695, stored for use on the hopefully soon-to-be-restored Swanage branch.

Items of Great Western rolling stock, mostly kept for reasons of use rather than sentiment, survive at a number of foreign preservation locations. Taking coaches first, your author must mention here that in his younger days he was employed as a pupil civil engineer on the Great Western Railway at Wolverhampton. While there he was sometimes instructed to accompany R. F. Wilson, the much venerated Divisional Engineer, on his tours of inspection in the then new engineer's inspection saloon No 80794. Never in his wildest dreams did he think that one day No 80794 would belong to him personally and he would invite people to join him on tours of inspection of one of England's premier tourist lines. The North Yorkshire Moors Railway, where this beautiful vehicle is kept, uses the saloon for entertaining VIP visitors.

A rather similar function is served by the VIP saloon No 9005, of 1930 vintage, stationed at Steamtown, Carnforth. Rather surprisingly the Midland Railway Centre at Butterley in Derbyshire – a real bastion of LMS railway engineering – includes GWR auto-trailer No 38 of 1907 among its assets. The Kent & East Sussex Railway at Tenterden has diesel railcar No 20 of the later Swindon-built trailer-hauling variety. The KESR used to have No 38 as well but this vehicle has not been seen recently.

Coming now to goods rolling stock, the ubiquitous Toad brake van is to be found on the Bluebell Railway, the Keighley & Worth Valley Railway, at Steamtown, the Chasewater Light Railway, Brownhills, West Midlands, and (in tool-van form) at the Conwy Valley Railway Museum, Bettws-y-Coed, North Wales. Also originally of North Wales domicile, but Swindon origin, are 2ft gauge slate trucks at Brockham Museum, Betchworth, Surrey and on the platform of the shortly-to-be-moved British Rail station at Blaenau Ffestiniog.

Fruit vans exist both on the North Norfolk Railway and the North Yorkshire Moors line; both these companies also have GWR open wagons, as does the Middleton Railway near Leeds which operated steam locomotives 12 years before the Stockton & Darlington Railway opened. The Middleton also has an ex-GWR steam crane made by Messrs T. Booth & Sons and dating from 1880. A tool van also built for breakdown work, belongs to the SR Q class locomotive fund and is located on the Bluebell Railway. Two bogie bolster wagons (Macaws) exist at the depot of the Scottish Railway Preservation Society at Falkirk, Scotland and nearly as far away from home territory is a 12-ton box van on the Lakeside Railway in Cumbria.

Overseas, we find a GWR corridor brake composite of 1938 which went to the famous Steamtown in Vermont, USA, an establishment which now has a dubious future. Journeying further afield still and really quite astonishing was the departure in 1977 of No 4079 *Pendennis Castle* for a place in the remote Outback of Western Australia. The newly-built town of Dampier was a terminal and port of the Hammersley Iron Propriety Ltd's Iron Ore line from mines a few hundred miles inland.

The Hammersley management, concerned that its staff would have little to do in their leisure hours, conceived the idea of having a steam locomotive on its ultra-modern railway; Hammersley came to Britain with the idea of buying an ex-London Midland & Scottish Black Five 4–6–0. History repeated itself in that, while at Steamtown, Carnforth, where three of these engines were based, an eloquent George Hinchcliffe, Manager of Flying Scotsman Enterprises, persuaded the Hammersley men to buy *Pendennis Castle* instead. So poor 'Pen', unloved, unwanted and imprisoned (for clearance reasons she was not normally allowed to run outside the depot) went into

109

exile in an inhospitable land, as far as possible from home, while remaining on the same planet.

However, an account published in *Railway World* for November 1979 indicates that this favourite among GWR locomotives is still with her admirers; enough of them exist down under to think nothing of chartering an aircraft to fly the 800 miles from Perth or the 2000 from Sydney to see her ladyship perform on the high iron of one of the world's newest and heaviest-worked railroads. There is even talk of having a go at beating the speed record for steam in Australia, using a 12-mile length of straight track on the Hammersley Iron Railway main line. The noble efforts of the Pilbarra Railway Historical Society to keep *Pendennis Castle* running in the long term are aided and abetted by the rainless climate of her new abode. It is also perhaps a point that the Southern Hemisphere might escape a possible nuclear holocaust.

This story of preservation in far away places ends with an enigma. In the Allied debacle of 1940, 35 of the legendary Dean Goods 0–6–0s were abandoned to Hitler's forces on the continent of Europe. The tale of their amazing wanderings – still to be chronicled – has no place here, but in 1946 some of the survivors were sent by the United Nations Relief and Rehabilitation Administration to another war in far-off China. For the record their numbers were 2392, 2393, 2432, 2439, 2462, 2465, 2477, 2486, 2477, 2557, 2566, 2571. The question is, after 30 years of peace in China, are any of them still in existence there? Even with new standard *steam* locomotives still leaving the erecting shop there in 1980 at the rate of 300 a year, so that old non-standard locomotives are becoming less likely to survive by the hour, it could well be that there is some corner of a vast nation where these tiny but excellent machines still serve a useful purpose.

17 GWR equipment still in service

So far we have looked at preserved GWR equipment. But much survives in everyday use as part of regular and continuing use even if, unlike the artifacts referred to in chapter 2, there is no intention of using them indefinitely.

In first place we must put that delightful creation, the Vale of Rheidol line, which is still wholly GWR apart from the colours; nevertheless we must pass quickly, on the grounds that the VoR is a borderline case and verging on preservation and is thus dealt with elsewhere. This disposes of the only Great Western line and trains still offering the same service to the public as they did before 1947.

The last standard gauge Great Western locomotives still in 'normal' commercial service on their own line seem to have been three 57XX pannier tanks (Nos 4646, 4696 and 9774) which worked in the Wrexham area as late as November 1966; this was a scant 10 years after 94XX 0–6–0T No 3409 had been completed at the Yorkshire Engine Co's works, Sheffield, in October 1956, the last locomotive of GWR design to be built. As regards rolling stock, the last passenger coaches to GW design were rather surprisingly a group of non-corridor brake composites, built very unusually by contractors R. Y. Pickering & Co in 1953. They formed five B sets in use in the Plymouth area until 1962. A few ex-GWR vehicles were, as this was written, still just in service with BR on parcels and freight trains, while a large number of GW vehicles of different kinds are used by the civil engineer and others.

Obsolete passenger carriages are often adapted for use as office accommodation workshops and mess vans and occasionally such items come up for sale; the BR stores controller who looks after scrap sales usually advises preservationists who might be interested. A recent occasion was the disbanding of a number of top-secret emergency control trains which produced several GWR carriage gems for preservation. As far as is known, only one standard gauge GW passenger coach is still in service (although not for public use) and is a singular vehicle in both senses of the word. This is the famous whitewash coach, which first saw the light of day as toplight brake third No 2360 at Swindon in 1911, but was converted for use as an experimental coach in 1932.

Those enviable people who spend their lives on the fascinating job of looking after railway permanent way naturally need checks on the quality of their work. An elegant piece of instrument-making known as a Hallade recorder – named after the French engineer whose invention it was – was used; this can be placed on the floor of a carriage and can record vertical and transverse oscillations in various directions while the vehicle moves along the line. A problem arises because some coaches ride well and others badly; in order to eliminate this variable, the GWR alone amongst the Big Four companies set aside an experimental coach, which was maintained as far as possible to a standard condition. Recordings were then made according to a programme which took No 2360 regularly on tours of inspection of all the main lines of the Great Western. As a result there was reasonable confidence that the result of one run would be comparable with the following one and thus provide useful material.

Three other advantages also accrued; since the alterations to the coach included the conversion of the van portion to an observation end, those directly responsible could be immediately confronted with any bad riding track encountered. Second, the location of any serious fault could be pin-pointed by a shot of white paint dropped on to the line through a simple automatically-operated whitewash valve. Thirdly, the car could be used for research into the riding qualities of new or modified bogies, by repeating runs over the same section of line with and without whatever new feature of the running gear was being investigated.

It was not only the high-ups and technical staff who came on the runs; those who normally work on the ground came too. It was the sort of arrangement which led to industrial relations of a quality which in retrospect one finds difficult to believe, in spite of experiencing them first-hand. Since one of 2360's outings normally covers the territory of a number of length gangs, its compartments (which remained intact after the conversion) came in useful to accommodate those waiting their turn.

112

Happily, even now 50 years later, 2360 (now DW 139) still watches over the quality of BR's Western Region track. The main change is that a black box has replaced the mechanical Hallade instrument.

This brings us to the greatest, biggest and almost totally unconsidered hunk of GW equipment still extant lying (literally) all around – the permanent way itself. On that fateful day of 31 December 1947 the GW handed on over 9,000 miles of track, with the trifling complication of 45,000 sets of switches and 53,000 crossings, common and obtuse. Correction, *no* obtuse crossings – the Great Western called them elbows. GWR permanent way was as original as the names used for its components or, for that matter, its locomotive fleet.

How much of the estimated $2\frac{1}{2}$ million tons of GWR pw material is still around is hard to estimate, but it will still be well into four figures in terms of miles laid. Although the old company in its last days dabbled a little reluctantly in flat-bottom rails and continuous welded rail, one is a little sorry that (for example) the Great Western Society does not use GW traditional track for running GW traditional trains inside its depot. From the outset GWR track was unconventional. Brunel proposed longitudinal timber baulks to carry the weight, with longitudinal flattish rails (known as bridge rail) to absorb the wear and distribute the load. The baulk road was abandoned for new work and renewals well before the end of the broad gauge in 1892 but, as related elsewhere, enough survived involuntarily to be recovered to form a noble exhibit at Didcot. Even after the second world war one could occasionally see the odd siding end with baulk road still in use.

Even when the more normal bull-head track was adopted, the GWR version was still far from conventional, but this time in detail rather than in principle. While other companies progressed from spikes and treenails to coach-screws and oak ferrules in fastening the chairs to sleepers, our company used bolts held by fang-nuts underneath. Later, chairbolts with the familiar square nuts on top came in but fittings (the GW term for point and crossing work) were always fanged. On plain line, chairs were held to gauge by a transverse saw-tooth adzing which fitted the shape of the underside of the chair; while the bolts were being tightened the chair was pressed down on to the sleeper with a force of several tons. The standard British 95 lb/yd bull-head main line rail was, amazingly, substituted for the traditional GWR 97½ lb/yd 'Ought-Ought' section in the 1920s, although a small quantity of OO was rolled each year for use in tunnels. GWR switches were also rather different from other people's, all being of the more robust 'joggled' pattern; the undercut switch was unknown. The standard switches also had curved instead of straight planing. Directly attached to some GWR switches were what are known as check-lumps and these were a unique GW speciality. By their means a check-rail could be led directly off the heel of the switch. Incidentally what other companies also knew as check rails – the short rails provided opposite crossings – were known on the GWR as guard rails.

Alas, the specially-tailored geometrically-designed big junction layouts can in no way have survived; even such a modest complication as a single compound (a non-GWR man would know one as a single slip) are rare on the normally simple layouts of preservation enterprises. All these things and many others are reasons why one might make an attempt to influence GW preservers (a) that just any old bit of track won't do but (b) that there is still plenty of true-blue material around, even if it might mean a little more trouble to find it.

One thing that is still specially conspicuous on many ex-Great Western routes is the distinctive semaphore signalling. One must salute the signal engineers of British Rail's Western Region for having held out against alien influences longer than any other department. To this day the department continues to use its own elegant but rather old-fashioned lower quadrant signals wherever mechanical signalling is still in service. The various preserved lines and museums have ample specimens of the various types of arm, post and bracket – even the otherwise totally American-style Forest (miniature) Railroad Park near Liskeard, Cornwall, had a GWR semaphore signal by the entrance; but what are likely to become just a memory are the great gantries at the approaches to such places as Shrewsbury, Taunton, Exeter, Newton Abbot and Plymouth. The days of these magnificent manifestations of the signal engineer's art are just now running out; their cousins elsewhere began to be replaced by colour-lights even in Great Western times and the process is now nearly at an end. Although, since it operates with only remote human intervention, signalling is the most realistic mechanical thing on the railway for reproduction in model form and one must hope that someone will save a great GW semaphore gantry in full size for posterity. There is still just time. While this

114

is not strictly within the realms of continued use hopefully one or other preserved line can sport a working Great Western automatic train control ramp near a distant signal to show how advanced the GWR was in 1906. The system lasted well over 50 years until replaced by electro-magnetic BR aws.

From the mechanical and electrical equipment involved in signalling one moves to various other GWR mechanical and electrical devices which still perform less glamorous but quite essential services for new owners. For example, the Great Western Railway was the largest owners of docks in Britain, with berths, piers, docks at Plymouth, Cardiff, Swansea, Newport, Barry, Port Talbot, Weymouth and even in London. Cranes, dock-gates, pumps, lifts, etc. abound in these places and, just as they do elsewhere in GWR territory, many of them are old enough to have been installed by the old company. One of the largest pumping stations in Britain copes with the legendary Great Spring which, 100 years ago, so hampered the boring of the Severn Tunnel. The bore would quickly flood if the pumps ceased work. On average some 20 million gallons are taken from below the river each day. Interestingly, the water does not come from the great river so close above, but from an independent, completely pure and eminently-saleable source. Preservers of unusual facts about GWR might treasure the thought that the resident engineer on this mighty project, Charles Richardson, was the inventor, designer and maker of the first modern cricket bat with spliced cane handle. At the other end of the scale and less dignified, but no less beneficial to past and present railway travellers, are the cisterns and plumbing of countless GWR spend-a-penny installations still open for custom, a very suitable point at which to end our review of the company's excellent equipment preserved by virtue of being both needed and in use.

18 A few failures

Since GWR preservation is so much a success story the failures that there have been stand out so much more vividly. But even with these tales of lost endeavours aside, one must additionally consider a few might-have-beens; things that could have been done if the preservers of the time had been on their toes. Then one must consider GWR preservation in quite general terms and discuss whether the great efforts which have been made do in any way fall short of their objectives.

For example, the biggest GWR locomotive collection, at Didcot, was praised for its comprehensiveness in respect of the fleet as a whole. But if one compares it with the types of locomotive actually allocated to Didcot in the Jubilee Year of 1935, the story is different. In those days the shed was a haven for smaller and older machinery and of 43 locomotives of 14 classes allocated, only two, the Hall and the 43XX classes, are there today; only two more, the Dean Goods and 2251 0–6–0s, can be still found elsewhere in the world. The main missing links are:

Duke class 4–4–0
Bulldog class 4–4–0
ex-Cambrian Railways 0–6–0
ex-Midland & South Western Junction 2–4–0
517 class 0–4–2T

There was also a collection of small elderly 0–6–0Ts much rebuilt but in origin dating from the days of Armstrong and Dean, used mostly for shunting in the adjoining Ordnance Depot. Some even had wide spark-arresting smokestacks. The somewhat similar 655, 1813, 1901 and 2021 classes were all represented and in addition there was even one 1076 class with outside cranks and frames as well as one other 1901 which had still kept its saddle tanks instead of the by then normal pannier type.

116

Assessing this 'non-preservation' to very strict standards by taking the Railway Correspondence & Travel Society's 12-volume *Locomotives of the Great Western Railway* (instead of the slim GWR Engine Book as we did before) as our counsel of perfection, there are (in addition to the above) only 11 more types of true (ie not absorbed) GWR locomotives in existence at close of play on 31 December, 1947, other than those above, which failed to be preserved. The biggest regret is one that has been mentioned before, the disappearance of a design which was a most important milestone in the whole long saga of British – not only Great Western – locomotive engineering, the Saints. The sad thing is that *Saint David* of the design in question, lasted as late as 1953 and, indeed, *Lady of Lynn* whose appearance with straight footplate approached more closely that of the class originally, survived well into 1952.

Again, tears must be shed at the demise of the huge and magnificent 47XX 2–8–0s which pioneered in Britain the use of eight-coupled locomotives for mixed traffic rather than freight. It is inconceivable to us now that they were allowed to vanish, particularly as they lasted into the beginning of the age of preservation in 1964. Alas, by chance, none of the nine was sold to Woodham Bros of South Wales, from whose scrapyard one might well have emerged.

Of the others, only the strange Aberdare 2–6–0s with inside cylinders and outside cranks, and the little Metro 2–4–0Ts fail to be represented by close relatives; the Hall class could, for example, stand in for the Counties and Granges, the 51XX and 45XX 2–6–2Ts for the 3150 and 44XX designs and the 16XX 0–6–0Ts for the 1854 and 2721 classes.

Without doubt, therefore, the failures of recent GW locomotive preservation are few indeed and most of them not of great importance. All the more, then, it shows up the almost complete failure to keep any locomotive of any of the types which ended their service before the old company was nationalised. In fact, 4–4–0 *City of Truro* stands quite alone in representing the hundreds of designs and types that had disappeared before 1948. One only has to think of what has survived of the past motive power of, say, the nineteenth century forerunners of the LMS and LNER to wonder why examples of treasures such as the French Compound 4–4–2s, the Badminton and Armstrong 4–4–0s or the famous Dean Singles, were not similarly saved. And as for the absence of anything broad-gauge, words fail . . .

Of course, there would be problems in assembling a comprehensive collection of Victorian GWR motive power, even allowing, as one must, for the acquisition of supernatural powers. Like most great human achievements, the superb standardised twentieth-century GW fleet was born out of Divine Discontent; in this case dissatisfaction with the highly non-standardised and mostly ramshackle machinery that preceded it. You would certainly need a very large museum indeed. Even when there was a fairly large class such as the 40 strong 3521 class, one might find that several exhibits would be needed, as follows:

(1) Broad gauge 0–4–2T, as built circa 1888
(2) Broad gauge 0–4–4T, after alteration circa 1890
(3) Narrow gauge 0–4–4T, after conversion in 1892
(4) Narrow gauge 4–4–0(!), after rebuilding circa 1900
(5) Narrow gauge 4–4–0, with No 3 taper boiler and large cab circa 1910

To replace these missing locomotives with full-size replicas would appear to be beyond the bounds of possibility, although it has been done in the case of some of the earliest (but also the smallest) steam locomotives. Replicas, of course, need not be full-size but this kind of preservation only preserves such abstract things as the shape and movement; it is called railway modelling. A glance at any of several periodicals such as *Railway Modeller* would show that excellent off-the-shelf mass-produced models of Great Western locomotives in 4mm–1ft scale – the most popular size – are available from many model shops at absurdly cheap prices. Virtually all the types which have got themselves preserved appear as ready-to-run models. But, much more important, models of many of the unpreserved ones are available as kits which require care rather than skill to produce an acceptable model. Included are the following:

De Glehn	4–4–2	Firefly (broad gauge)	2–2–2
County class	4–4–0	1334	2–4–0
County class	4–6–0	Birdcage	2–4–2T
Saint class	4–6–0	1804	0–6–0T
Grange class	4–6–0	1854	0–6–0T
47XX class	2–8–0	2021	0–6–0T
Aberdare	2–6–0	Rhymney AP	0–6–2T
Standard Goods	0–6–0	Rhymney A1	0–6–2T
Beyer Peacock	0–6–0		
Bulldog	4–4–0		
Duke	4–4–0		

A short distance from Great Western Society HQ at Didcot in the village of Long Wittenham (take a local train to Appleford Halt) is a public model landscape and railway called Pendon. The ambience is mostly GWR and is as close as one can get to such failures of preservation as a Brunel timber viaduct, as well as various long lost GWR locomotives and trains. The attention to detail is such that the ticket collectors in the corridors of the 1:76 scale expresses carry in their buttonholes authentic representations of the red rose which it was the custom of this elite corps to wear when carrying out their duties.

Larger models can give the possibility of preserving the way a locomotive functions as well as the way it looks. In $3\frac{1}{2}$in gauge and upwards a steam locomotive can go by real steam generated by a proper coal fire; it can even be driven from a flat car behind. The time and skill needed to produce such a model from castings and raw material is increased ten or twenty-fold compared with making a little one from a kit, but designs and descriptions for many of the unpreserved GWR types exist. Don Young's *Saint David* and 4–4–0 *County Carlow*, Keith Wilson's Bulldog (currently in progress), Martin Evans' Metro Tank, J. N. Maskelyne's Standard Goods and LBSC's *Purley Grange* are just a few that have appeared in the *Model Engineer*.

Live steam Kings, Halls, Manors, pannier tanks and Dean singles in these sizes far exceed the numbers that existed for real, while dozens of *The Great Bear* 4–6–2s keep alive the one famous prototype; it has been noted earlier that Didcot provides facilities for running live steam passenger-hauling models.

The fact that early coaches had a certain survival value in such roles as chicken huts has meant that enough nineteenth century Great Western coach bodies have survived to make one day a reasonable showing; even before restoration they are like great-grandfather's hammer – only three new heads and five new handles! Amongst the twentieth century's proliferation of carriage design, to have failed to secure an example of only two out of the ten main design families is no disgrace. What is cause for regret is the absence of three particular GW specialities, viz, slip carriages, standard 70ft coaches, and (very odd for a line with such feudal ideas) one of the classless end-kitchen dining cars. In fact, the preservation of a standard 70ft concertina luncheon and tea car – the most numerous of all the types of GWR dining car because the general introduction of restaurant cars coincided with the concertina period of construction in 1906–07 – would have killed several birds with one brick. In fact, most of these vehicles survived well into the preservation era. Of course there are standard-gauge railway preservation organisations in the world who are sufficiently prosperous financially to commission new carriage bodies to old designs – an example is the Strasburg Railroad in Pennsylvania, USA – so perhaps all may not be lost for ever. The end-kitchen diner of 1932 at York is not one of these, for it is a composite with both first- and third-class sections. Most of the GWR composite dining cars had kitchens in the centre and this type is yet another gap in the carriage relics.

Two more families of GWR wheeled equipment, very different but serving the same role, are also absent. The famous group of 100 steam rail motors dating from 1903 to 1907 had their engines removed in the 1920s, so becoming auto-trailers. In consequence none of the 22 designs there were (plus numerous others from the absorbed lines) have survived, although their successors, the Great Western diesel railcars of the 1930s are well covered, as we have seen. For many years the GWR extended its network by a fleet of what were called road motors but which any person other than a GW enthusiast would call motor buses. None of these has come down to us either, although one or two of the same models used by other operators are in the hands of commercial road vehicle preservers.

So much for failures in rolling stock; now let us consider failures of location. With GWR preserved lines and museum depots both widespread and numerous there is no question of any failure in principle, except that no one has yet preserved a *junction*. However, one or two failures of specific projects can be mentioned. The 12-mile Brent to Kingbridge branch which was the first GWR line proposed for preservation, had an edge over neighbour Dart Valley in that at Brent station the branch had its own independent platform and could have been operated separately from the main line. On the other hand, South Brent being a small village, the station's *raison d'etre* was wholly due to the branch and as the tourist operation might not have generated sufficient interchange with the ten sparse and now non-existent stopping trains on the main-line to justify their continuation. Even in the 1920s the through Kingsbridge coach from Paddington was slipped from the Cornish Riviera Express at Exeter, and worked forward to Brent on a local, before being sent down to Kingsbridge on the branch train. By the time it

120

arrived the main train would be many miles further on nearing St Austell in Cornwall.

As at Buckfastleigh, there was also the problem (then unsuspected) of the reconstruction of the A38 trunk road, which was to cross the site of the branch a short distance south of the junction with the main line. All in all the substitution of the shorter Buckfastleigh line seems a fair exchange.

A serious tear must be shed because the scheme to give *Pendennis Castle* a home which was the locomotive equivalent of a country cottage came to naught. The tiny modern locomotive depot at Market Overton, Leicestershire, was small, handy for *Pendennis'* dedicated group of volunteers and had attached to it and available a well-laid non-public railway line of ample length, almost completely free from the possibility of bureaucratic interference. The door was open to a type of steam operation without which the world is certainly the poorer.

Looking round railway preservation, it seems that so many of those involved are in the position of he who mounts a tiger and cannot dismount. The idea behind Market Overton was a steam centre that could, as it were, heave-to during financial storms but give pleasant go-as-you-please railway yachting at other times. Open days could be held to assist the funds but not if the yacht needed repairs. Then the crew would have to get down to it, and certainly, the captain could be relied upon to do more than his share of the less attractive tasks.

In the end a whole series of circumstances combined to make this non-ambitious but otherwise perfect scheme a dream. The acquisition of *Flying Scotsman* (plus the services of its full-time manager) by Bill McAlpine, doubts over the retention of one BR connection and heavy costs involved in putting in another, were some of them. So *Pendennis Castle* was taken to Steamtown, Carnforth, but not until after a difference of opinion as to whether the move had been agreed to by the principals in the affair, which led to her being welded to the rails at Market Overton!

Little is now heard of a scheme to preserve the branch from Swindon to Highworth, although there are more promising noises coming from those involved in the nearby proposal to revive the old Midland & South Western Junction line from Swindon six miles northwards to Cricklade. But since the track alone, even at scrap prices would cost (say) some £20,000 a mile and that would only be a fraction of the overall expense involved,

121

one cannot easily be sanguine about this project contributing seriously to the Cause in the future. Another scheme which failed involved several ex-GWR roadbeds at Cymmer in the once coal-rich Afan Valley above Port Talbot; it might be a pointer to the future in that the idea was to revive the memory of a collection of long-lost (but not, alas, Great Western) narrow-gauge locomotive treasures by creating half-size replicas.

Of failures in principle one can think of two, both alas concerning thrilling and exciting features of the old Great Western. Never again will anyone stand beside the railway at a set of water troughs and enjoy the excitement of watching a fast-running express pick up water. Oddly enough, early BR diesels needed the troughs because they had water scoops to pick-up water for the train heating boilers; later, a change to electric heating made the troughs obsolete. Never, again, too, will anyone see an express slip a coach at a station at which the train does not stop. Incidentally, the south side of the main line just west of Didcot station was one of the best places to see this peculiarly Great Western operation.

Lastly (and not unexpectedly) one has to record the failure to preserve any of the fine GWR ships which, although they never managed to travel so far away as GWR locomotives, were responsible for many great deeds in war and gave good service in peace. The last of them, the *St Patrick*, went on in 1965 to offer Greek Island cruises under the name *Thermopylae*, but all the others (except possibly one or two hulks on ex GWR canals) have ended their time at the breakers.

Above: Great Western steam in action on BR with an immaculate No 6000 *King George V* seen here leaving Hope-under-Dinmore tunnel north of Hereford with the northbound Deeside Venturer in October 1980. *G. F. Heiron*

Below: Severn Valley Railway: No 7819 *Hinton Manor* enters Arley station with the GWR Society's vintage train in September 1979. *Michael Baker*

Above: SVR's 57XX 0-6-0PT No 5764 leaves Bewdley with a special train including a former GW special saloon. *Author's collection*

Below: Bewdley station in 1979 with GW 0-6-0ST No 813 in the background and post-war corridor third in the foreground. *G. F. Heiron*

19 Steam operation today and tomorrow

Any machine that has moving parts capable of rapid movement and weighs 50 tons or more is liable to be expensive to maintain. The steam locomotive is no exception, even though ton-for-ton its simplicity makes it cheaper to repair than other types of prime mover, provided that the set-up for doing those repairs is on a reasonably equal basis. Of course, the set-up for maintaining a preserved locomotive fleet formed of many locomotive classes, compared with a working fleet of very few (of whatever type) cannot be on the same basis. It is certainly an advantage that much of the labour involved in keeping steam, especially Great Western steam, is offered free, but this is far more than balanced by the fact that any new parts needed are a matter of expensive custom engineering.

So far, volunteers have always succeeded in confounding those (mostly professionals) who call themselves realists, (and whom the volunteers would call pessimists) in the jobs they have managed to tackle. But always there comes the question – is there a limit? And even if the real limit has not yet been reached, is there also the prospect of our play-safe bureaucracy imposing an artificial limit to what a particular group of people may try and do? As a result of two accidents a few years ago, one of which was attributed to an amateur approach to the black art of boiler maintenance, this has already begun to happen.

In due time though, really major repair problems will arise, such as the need for complete boiler renewals. Until now the preservationists have coped with renewing the more delicate internal parts such as flues, tubes, stays and even tube-plates. But the time will come when the only possibility of putting a locomotive back into service will be by ordering a new boiler, at a sum which might reasonably be not far short of £100,000. The same kind of arguments apply to other portions of a locomotive when they become worn out. In fact, several preserved locomotives have already been laid aside, or turned into static exhibits, because this sort of treatment is now necessary.

In respect of main-line running, the situation has been made worse by the fact that, like human beings, occasional strenuous days out in the hills followed by long sedentary periods at home is not good for the health of steam locomotives. Put another way, intermittent use has meant a very high cost per mile run because so much of steam locomotive maintenance expenditure is needed regardless of whether the engine is out running or not. Without becoming too discouraging, may one suggest that any person who wishes to find out more about the problems encountered is recommended to do so at first hand by joining a group involved in locomotive preservation, or, failing that, read about it in Bill Harvey's definitive *Manual of Steam Locomotive Restoration and Preservation* (David & Charles 1980). Nevertheless, in spite of all the difficulties, the devotion of the staff and volunteers has been such that it has been very rare, so far, for any of the preservation groups to fail to meet the promises inherent in their published timetables or announcements. So far, also, there have been no significant closures or bankruptcies among them, although I have a suspicion that one or two have once or twice come close to disaster in this way, and one or two of the less financially sound schemes might yet founder.

In spite of it all, most of the objectives of what was proposed 12 years ago for steam on a steamless British Rail have been achieved; although the costs shown in the Appendix to this book will bring out wry smiles. Even so, this controversial proposal to put BR into showbiz has in no way been a runaway bonanza. One group for whom it has not been at all good are the locomotive owners; like so many things, the reason is very clear if one does a little simple arithmetic. For example, when *Clun Castle* made all that running on the Eastern Region in 1967, the fare asked for a day out was £6 from London. Since then costs have gone up four times, but it is not at all possible to fill a series of trains at four times the 1967 fare, that is £24; £15 is more usual today and the shortfall is made up by those who provide the steam and so put on the play.

But there is another and more fundamental problem as well. Carrying the theatrical analogy a little further, the Steamy Train Show has the elements of putting on a play in a theatre in which the audience is not charged for admission. Only a chosen few pay for the privilege of being back-stage during the performance where, although they see the stars close-up behind the scenes, there is only an oblique and half-blind glimpse of the performance. Put another way, when you travel in a train you cannot see it; and if you do go to see it, Messrs Ford, Kodak and Shell, etc, rather than those who run the train, get the money.

The two Great Western vintage main-line trains fielded by the Great Western Society and the Severn Valley Railway respectively, until recently, did something to give a better balance between what was offered to the payers and what was offered to the non-payers. The payers at least enjoyed travel à la GWR, even if they saw little of the green brassy monster up front. Alas, new regulations for the running of private rolling stock promulgated in late 1979 have made it uneconomic at present to maintain a main-line vintage train for BR operation, certainly so far as the Great Western Society is concerned. The SVR has not yet declared its hand in this matter; it may be that the enforcement of the new regulations is not so serious a matter when concerned with a set of coaches likely to be used for 100 and more days a year on a working railway in addition to its forays out on to BR. In addition, one day, perhaps, BR will accept the notion of charging less to those who bring their own trains, instead of more.

But change is imminent, mainly because in this connection, almost literally, the days of the vacuum brake on BR are numbered. All new rolling stock for some years has had air brakes only and all too soon the only carriage sets available, fitted with brakes compatible to those on GWR locomotives, will be privately preserved. Moreover, BR will not own any locomotives which can be used on preserved carriages. Of course, solutions are possible – one has only to remember that *King George V* worked air-braked trains in the USA during 1927 and, indeed, before the 1923 grouping standardised the vacuum brake in Britain, the GWR kept a little clutch of locomotives fitted for working air-braked trains from other companies' lines. In addition, there were carriages with dual brakes to cover through working on to certain 'foreign' territory. Even so, before a solution is found, no doubt the official 'too difficult' brigade will have a field day first.

Both the forms of main-line steam operation recommended at the outset can still be found in Britain. Alas, the first, for which the steam owners, now compulsorily banded together under the title Steam Locomotive Owners Association or SLOA, charter trains and sell the seats to railway enthusiasts, is the only one which is practised in GW territory. This is a pity, for the other sort, in which British Railways schedules regular steam trains for holiday-makers and hires steam locomotives to haul them, is usually a better bargain for both the owners and BR. It is a double pity, when one considers how many popular seaside and other holiday resorts once filled the pages of the GWR's own famous *Holiday Haunts* book.

Careful consideration of all such places fails to reveal one which would be suitable. One problem is that in their enthusiasm for disposing of everything concerned with steam, BR's then management scrapped the majority of turntables, regardless of the fact that another lot of BR managers were working on a project to introduce locomotives which needed turning – the power cars of the High Speed Trains. True, they only needed turning, and then only sometimes, when a power car needs replacement but even so turntables would have been worth retaining at a few more places.

It seems feasible though to introduce a particular steam operation which has excellent revenue potential, breaks no railway rules, is perfectly situated in respect of the largest GWR depot and has locomotive turning facilities at both ends. Best of all, you would need to pay to see more than a glimpse of the show. The proposal is that the GW Society should provide a steam locomotive and either BR or the GW Society a set of vehicles (which need not necessarily be passenger-carrying) to make several return trips on the miles of relief lines between Didcot and Reading, the locomotive turning on the triangle at the latter and on the GWS turntable at the former.

The action would be viewed and recorded from a moving grandstand in the form of another train running alongside on the parallel line of this four-track section. Days of light traffic such as Saturdays outside the holiday season and Sundays on pre-arranged dates, or at times when the engineering department did not have possession of the lines in question, would be best both from the operating point of view. Window seats on the north side of the grandstand train might command a premium and stock with opening top-light windows would be used. Speeds of both trains would vary so that all customers got a proper view as the two trains passed and re-passed. Of course, it would be the deliberate staging of something that frequently used to happen just by chance; but one remembers that when it did one got unparalleled sight and sound of the majesty of steam in action.

128

Tickets would normally include going one way by steam and one way by the grandstand train.

This is perhaps a slightly startling proposal, but has its place here in emphasising that some very hard, original and imaginative thinking will have to be done if steam operation at more than the sedate speeds of preserved light railway running is to continue. Hope lies in the fact that imaginative thinking was always (or nearly always) a feature of the old GWR and this is one thing that has been passed on down to the new Great Western; one example was that the Great Western Society made a day for the media by inviting a famous disc jockey to do the first turn on a new *locomotive* turntable!

20 A review of achievement

The purpose of this last chapter is to look in a factual way across the board at the progress of the Cause. That is to say, instead of discussing individual projects, the overall effort made is considered. First the sites; Table 1 lists all the known sites of GWR preservation effort which go beyond small relics. They are shown in what is basically their order of significance within geographical regions. The map reference given is the Ordnance Survey co-ordinate except in the case of sites outside Britain where latitude and longitude are used. Of course, it must be emphasised that in no way does an entry here imply that the site in question is open to the public, but most of them are.

Table 1 GREAT WESTERN PRESERVATION SITES

Note: figures given relate only to GWR items.

	Ordnance Survey Co-ordinates	See Chapters	Route Mileage	Locomotives, Rail Cars	Carriages	Wagons, Vans, Cranes, etc.	Stations, Depots Preserved
SOUTH WESTERN LOCATIONS							
Great Western Society Museum, Didcot	SU 524906	3, 4, 5	—	21	42	32	1
Dart Valley Railway { Buckfastleigh, Devon	SX 747663	7, 8	14½	12	15	18	5
Dart Valley Railway { Paignton, Devon	SX 889606	7, 8					
Great Western Railway Museum, Swindon, Wiltshire	SU 145846	15	—	5	—	—	—
West Somerset Railway, Minehead, Somerset	SS 984464	14	20	5	3	3	1
Great Western Preservation Group, Southall, London	TQ 368793	15	—	3	—	—	1
Science Museum, London	SS 960127	15	—	1	—	—	—
Tiverton, Devon	ST 670705	15	—	1	—	—	—
Bristol Suburban Railway, Avon	SK 014580	15	—	—	—	3	—
Cornish Steam Society, Bugle, Cornwall	ST 583722	15	—	—	1	1	—
Bristol Industrial Museum, Avon		15	—	—	1	2	—
Taff Vale Restorations, Bath		15	—	—	1	—	—
Kennet & Avon Canal	—	14	60	—	—	—	—
East Somerset Railway, Cranmore, Somerset	ST 664429	15	1¼	—	—	—	—
Lappa Valley Railway, near Newquay, Cornwall	SW 839564	9	1⅞	—	—	—	—
Pendon Museum, Long Wittenham, Oxfordshire	SU 532945	18		models only			
Fawley Hill Railway, near Henley-on-Thames, Oxfordshire		15	—	—	—	2	—
Plym Valley Railway, Plymouth	—	14	—	—	—	—	—
LOCATIONS IN WALES							
Vale of Rheidol, Aberystwyth	SN 587812	9	13	3	18	11	5
Welshpool & Llanfair Railway, Gwynedd	SJ 107069	9	8	2	—	8	2
Corris Railway Society, Corris, Gwynedd	SH 760075	9	1	—	—	4	1
Llangollen Railway Society	SJ 211423	15	—	1	1	6	2

	Ordnance Survey Co-ordinates	See Chapters	Route Mileage	Locomotives, Rail Cars	Carriages	Wagons, Vans, Cranes, etc.	Stations, Depots Preserved
Gwili Railway, Bronwydd Arms, Carmarthen	SN 417239	15	$1\frac{1}{4}$	1	1	—	1
Caerphilly Railway Society	ST 163865	15	$\frac{1}{2}$	1	—	4	—
9642 Group, NCB, Maesteg	SS 848915	15	—	1	—	2	—
National Museum of Wales, Cardiff	ST 192745	15	—	—	—	1	—
Pembrokeshire County Museum, Scotton	SM 991222	15	—	1	—	—	—
Railway Club of Wales, Swansea	SS 659927	15	—	—	—	1	—
GW Steam Preservation Group, Swansea	—	15	—	1	—	—	—
Festiniog Railway, Blaenau Ffestiniog, Gwynedd	SH 705460	9	$\frac{1}{8}$	—	—	2	—
Bala Lake (Lyn Tegid) Railway, Bala, Gwynedd	SH 881300	9	$4\frac{1}{2}$	—	—	—	1
Welsh Highland Railway, Porthmadog, Gwynedd	SH 567393	9	$\frac{1}{2}$	—	1	—	—
Brecon Mountain Railway, near Merthyr	SO 063120	9	$5\frac{1}{2}$	—	—	—	—
Teifi Valley Railway, Henllan, Dyfed	SN 358406	9	9	—	—	—	2
Talyllyn Railway, Tywyn, Gwynedd	SH 590008	9	—	2	1	8	—
Conwy Valley Railway Museum, Bettws-y-Coed	SH 796565	16	—	—	1	1	—
Woodham Bros, Barry, Glamorgan	ST 111670	15	(locomotives on hand as scrap)				
Powys County Council, Highways Department	SO 010425	20	4	—	—	—	—
Brecon & Abergavenny Canal	—	14	33	—	—	—	—

MIDLAND LOCATIONS

Severn Valley Railway, Bewdley	SO 715926	12, 13	$12\frac{1}{2}$	17	26	37	6
Dean Forest Railway, Norchard, Glos.	SO 629044	14	$4\frac{1}{2}$	5	2	13	4
Birmingham Railway Museum	SP 105841	10	—	10	2	9	1
Bulmers of Hereford	SO 505402	11	—	2	—	5	—

MIDLAND LOCATIONS (cont.)

Location	Ordnance Survey Co-ordinates	See Chapters	Route Mileage	Locomotives, Rail Cars	Carriages	Wagons, Vans, Cranes, etc.	Stations, Depots Preserved
Cambrian Railway Society, Oswestry, Salop	SJ 294297	15	—	1	—	1	—
Telford Steam Trust	SJ 675073	15	$\frac{1}{2}$	1	—	—	—
Dowty Railway Society, Ashchurch, Glos.	SO 925335	15	—	—	2	2	—
Stratford Canal	—	14	$25\frac{1}{2}$	—	—	—	—

FOREIGN LOCATIONS

Location	Ordnance Survey Co-ordinates	See Chapters	Route Mileage	Locomotives, Rail Cars	Carriages	Wagons, Vans, Cranes, etc.	Stations, Depots Preserved
Quainton Railway Centre, near Aylesbury	SP 739190	16	—	4	1	2	—
National Railway Museum, York	SE 594519	15	—	1	3	5	—
North Yorkshire Moors Railway, Pickering	SE 797842	16	—	1	1	3	—
Great Central Railway, Loughborough	SK 543194	16	—	2	—	—	—
Keighley & Worth Valley Railway, Haworth	SE 034371	16	—	2	—	1	—
Bluebell Railway, Sheffield Park, Sussex	TQ 403238	16	—	1	—	1	—
Hammersley Iron Railway, Western Australia	20.45S, 116.10E	16	—	1	—	—	—
Steamtown Museum, Carnforth, Lancashire	SD 496708	16	—	1	1	1	—
Steamport Museum, Southport, Lancashire	SD 341161	16	—	—	—	—	—
Steamtown, Bellows Falls, Vermont, USA	43.08N, 72.28W	16	—	1	1	1	—
Leicester Transport Museum	SK 589067	16	—	1	—	—	—
Kent & East Sussex Railway, Tenterden, Kent	TQ 882336	16	—	—	—	—	—
Midland Railway Centre, Butterley, Derbyshire	SK 403520	16	—	—	1	—	—
Mid-Hants Railway, Alresford, Hampshire	SU 588325	16	—	—	—	1	—
Brockham Museum, Betchworth, Surrey	TQ 198510	9	—	—	—	—	—
North Norfolk Railway, Sheringham	TG 156430	16	—	—	—	2	—
Middleton Railway, Leeds	SE 302309	16	—	—	—	2	—

	Ordnance Survey Co-ordinates	See Chapters	Route Mileage	Locomotives, Rail Cars	Carriages	Wagons, Vans, Cranes, etc.	Stations, Depots Preserved
Scottish RPS, Bo'ness, West Lothian	NS 995810	16	—	—	—	2	—
Lakeside & Haverthwaite Railway, Windermere	SD 349843	16	—	—	—	1	—
Chasewater Railway, Brownhills, Cannock	SK 034070	16	—	—	—	1	—
Peak Park Railway, Buxton (locomotives not yet on site)	—	16	—	2	—	—	—

Second, we consider the locomotives. Table 2 lists all (or hopefully all) GWR locomotives which, at the end of 1980, were in the hands of people who had the intention of restoring them. It is likely that some of these enterprises will fall by the wayside before then, but no doubt others will have been added to the list before publication. Certainly, there will be some changes of ownership and location to record.

A distinction is made between locomotives reported to be in working order, where the entry is made in heavy type, and others. Naturally the term 'working order' does not imply continual readiness for steam at a few hours notice; the category includes locomotives laid off for some temporary attention.

Table 2 PRESERVED GREAT WESTERN LOCOMOTIVES

Locomotives known to be operational at the time of writing are shown in **heavy type**.
Numbers and names allocated by owners subsequent to the GWR (including allocations by BR) shown in brackets.
Builders – Swindon Works except where stated otherwise.

(a) Tender Locomotives

No.	Name	Date	Present Location & Owner	Notes
King class 4-cyl 4–6–0				
6000	**King George V**	**1927**	**Bulmers, Hereford; NRM**	Static exhibit
6024	King Edward I	1930	Quainton Railway Society; 6024 PS	
			(also 6023 presently at Woodhams, Barry)	
Castle class 4-cyl 4–6–0				
4073	Caerphilly Castle	1023	Science Museum; NRM	
4079	**Pendennis Castle**	**1924**	**Hammersley Iron Railway**	
			Western Australia	
5029	Nunney Castle	1934	GWS, Didcot	
5051	**Drysllwyn Castle**	**1936**	**GWS, Didcot**	
	alias **Earl Bathurst**			
(7027)	(Thornbury Castle)	1949	Birmingham Railway Museum	
(7029)	**(Clun Castle)**	**1950**	**Birmingham Railway Museum**	
			(also 5043, 5080 at Birmingham Railway Museum for spare parts)	
Star class 4-cyl 4–6–0				
4003	Lode Star	1907	GWR Museum, Swindon	Static exhibit
Hall class 2-cyl 4–6–0				
4920	Dumbleton Hall	1929	Dart Valley Railway; DHPS	

No.	Name	Date	Present Location & Owner	Notes
4930	**Hagley Hall**	**1929**	**Severn Valley Railway**	
4942	Maindy Hall	1929	GWS, Didcot	
4979	Wootton Hall	1930	Quainton Railway Society	
4983	Albert Hall	1931	Birmingham Railway Museum; A.H. Ltd.	
5900	**Hinderton Hall**	**1931**	**GWS, Didcot**	
5952	Cogan Hall	1935	Cogan Hall Preservation Society	
6960	**Raveningham Hall**	**1944**	**Severn Valley Railway, private**	
(6989)	(Wightwick Hall)	1949	Quainton Railway Society	
(6990)	(Witherslack Hall)	1949	Great Central Railway: WHLS	
(6998)	**(Burton Agnes Hall)**	**1949**	**GWS, Didcot**	
4979	Wootton Hall	1930	Quainton Railway Society	
			(also at Barry 4936, 4953, 5967, 5972, 6984, 7903, 7927)	

Manor class 2-cyl 4–6–0

No.	Name	Date	Present Location & Owner	Notes
7807	**Cookham Manor**	**1938**	**GWS, Didcot**	
7812	**Erlestoke Manor**	**1939**	**Severn Valley Railway; E.M. Fund**	
7819	**Hinton Manor**	**1939**	**Severn Valley Railway**	
7820	(Dinmore Manor)	1950	Gwili Railway	
(7824)	(Foxcote Manor)	1950	Oswestry; Cambrian Railway Society	
(7827)	**(Lydham Manor)**	**1950**	**Dart Valley Railway**	
			(also at Barry 7802, 7821, 7828)	

City class double-framed 4–4–0

No.	Name	Date	Present Location & Owner	Notes
3717	City of Truro	1903	GWR Museum, Swindon; NRM	Static exhibit

Dukedog or Earl class double-framed 4–4–0

No.	Name	Date	Present Location & Owner	Notes
3217	**(Earl of Berkeley)**	**1938**	**Bluebell Railway; T.R.Gomm**	

No.	Name	Date	Present Location & Owner	Notes
28XX class 2-cyl 2–8–0				
2807		1905	GWPG, Southall	
2818		1905	National Railway Museum	Static exhibit
2857		**1918**	**Severn Valley Railway**	
2885		1938	GWPG, Southall	
3822		1940	GWS. Didcot	
(also at Barry 2859, 2861, 2873, 2874, 3802, 3803, 3814, 3845, 3850, 3855, 3862)				
43XX class 2-cyl 2–6–0				
5322		**1917**	**GWS, Didcot**	
9303 (alias 7325)		1937	Severn Valley Railway	
2251 class inside-cyl 0–6–0				
3205		**1946**	**Severn Valley Railway; D. Rouse**	
Dean Goods class inside-cyl 0–6–0				
2516		1887	GWR Museum, Swindon, NRM	Static exhibit
Stanier LMS class 8F 2–8–0				
(8431)		1944	Keighley & Worth Valley Railway	Built to order of Ministry of Supply
Stephenson Patentee 2–2–2				
— North Star		1935	GWR Museum, Swindon	Replica of 1837 original

No.	Name	Date	Present Location & Owner	Notes
(b) Tank Locomotives				
51XX class 2-cyl 2–6–2T				
4110		1936	GWPS, Southall	
4121		1937	Dean Forest Railway	
4141		**1946**	**Severn Valley Railway**	
4144		1946	GWS, Didcot	
4150		1947	Severn Valley Railway	
(4160)		1948	Birmingham Railway Museum	
5164		1930	Severn Valley Railway	
5193		1934	Steamport, Southport	
61XX class 2-cyl 2–6–2T				
6106		**1931**	**GWS, Didcot** (also at Barry 4115, 4156, 5199)	
42XX class 2-cyl 2–8–0T				
4247		1916	Peak Railway Society, Buxton	
4270		1919	GWSPG, Swansea	
5224		1924	Great Central Railway; private	
5239	**(Goliath)**	**1924**	**Dart Valley Railway**	
		(also at Barry 4248, 4253, 4277, 5227)		
72XX class 2-cyl 2–8–2T				
7200		1934	Quainton Railway Society	
7202		1934	GWS, Didcot	
			(also at Barry 7229)	

No.	Name	Date	Present Location & Owner	Notes
45XX class 2-cyl 2–6–2T				
4555		1924	Dart Valley Railway	
4561		1924	West Somerset Railway	
4566		**1924**	**Severn Valley Railway**	
4588		**1927**	**Dart Valley Railway**	
5521		1927	Dean Forest Railway	
5523		1927	Dean Forest Railway	
5541		**1928**	**Dean Forest Railway**	
5542		1928	West Somerset Railway	
5572		1929	GWS, Didcot	
		(also at Barry 5526, 5532, 5538, 5539, 5552, 5553)		
56XX class inside-cyl 0–6–2T				
5619		**1925**	**Telford Steam Trust**	
5637		1925	Birmingham Railway Museum	
5643		1925	Steamtown, Carnforth	
6619		1927	North Yorkshire Moors Railway	
6634		1928	GWPG, Southall	
6697		**1928**	**GWS, Didcot** (Builder: 6697 – Armstrong Whitworth)	
		(also at Barry 5668, 6634, 6686, 6695)		
57XX class inside-cyl 0–6–0T				
3650		**1939**	**GWS, Didcot**	
3738		**1937**	**GWS, Didcot**	
5764		**1929**	**Severn Valley Railway**	
5775		**1929**	**Keighley & Worth Valley Railway**	Runs as L89
5786			**Bulmers, Hereford; Worc. RS**	
7714		1930	Severn Valley Railway	Built Kerr Stuart

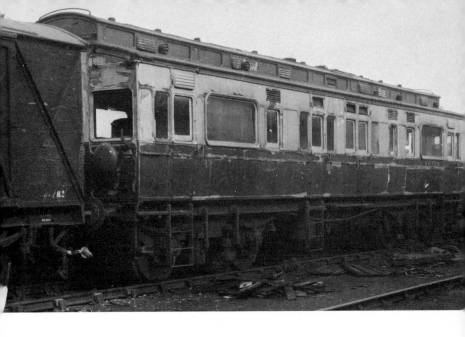

Above: Ashchurch: former GW clerestory engineer's saloon No 9044 seen after withdrawal from BR and before restoration by the Dowty Railway Preservation Society. *Author's collection*

Below: Great Western on the Metropolitan & Great Central: at Quainton steam centre 57XX 0-6-0PT No 7715, seen here in London Transport colours, is in action on an open day. *Eric Knight*

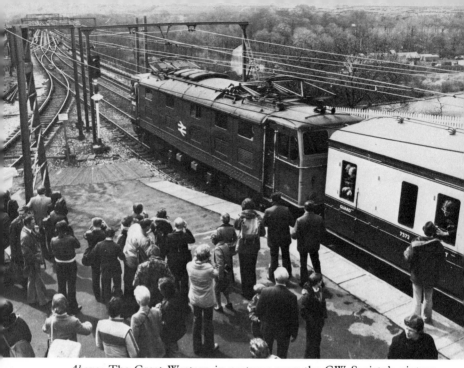

Above: The Great Western in pastures new: the GW Society's vintage train arrives at Dinting on 22 April 1979 behind dc electric locomotive No 76046. *Michael Baker*

Below: The Great Western in pictures: 2-6-0 No 5322 is seen at Marylebone with GW coaches for filming Walt Disney's *One of our Dinosaurs is Missing*, on 8 August 1974. *GW Society*

No.	Name	Date	Present Location & Owner	Notes
7715		**1930**	**Quainton Railway Society**	**Built Kerr Stuart**
7752		**1930**	**Birmingham Railway Museum**	**Built North British**
7754		1930	Llangollen Railway	
7760		**1930**	**Birmingham Railway Museum**	
9600		1945	Birmingham Railway Museum	
9642		1946	National Coal Board, Maesteg	
9681		1949	Dean Forest Railway (also at Barry 4612, 9629, 9682)	
94XX class inside-cyl 0–6–0T				
9400		1947	Swindon Museum	
9466		1952	Quainton Railway Society	
64XX class inside-cyl 0–6–0T				
6412		**1934**	**West Somerset Railway**	
6430		1937	Dart Valley Railway	
6435		1937	Dart Valley Railway	
15XX class 2-cyl 0–6–0T				
1501		1949	Severn Valley Railway; Warwicks RS	
16XX class 2-cyl 0–6–0T				
(1638)		**1951**	**Dart Valley Railway**	
14XX class inside-cyl 0–4–2T				
1420		1933	Dart Valley Railway	
1442		1934	Tiverton Museum	
1450		**1935**	**Dart Valley Railway**	
1466		1936	GWS, Didcot	

No.	Name	Date	Present Location & Owner	Notes
1361 class 2-cyl 0–6–0T				
1363		**1910**	**GWS, Didcot**	
1366 class 2-cyl 0–6–0T				
1369		1934	Dart Valley Railway	
Vale of Rheidol 2-cyl 2–6–2T				
7	**Owain Glyndŵr**	**1923**	**Aberystwyth; BR**	**Built by**
8	**Llywelyn**	**1923**	**Aberystwyth; BR**	**Davies & Metcalfe,**
9	**Prince of Wales**	**1902**	**Aberystwyth; BR**	**rebuilt Swindon**
Taff Vale inside-cyl 0–6–2T				
450	(ex-O1 class No 28)	1897	Caerphilly; National Museum	Built Neilson
426	(ex-O2 class No 85)	1899	Keighley & Worth Valley Railway	Built TVR Caerphilly
Welshpool & Llanfair 2-cyl 0–6–0T				
822	**The Earl**	**1903**	**Welshpool & Llanfair Railway**	**Built Beyer Peacock**
823	The Countess	1903	NRM: Welshpool & Llanfair Railway	Built Beyer Peacock
ex-Corris Railway Locomotives 2-cyl 0–4–2ST				
3	**(Sir Haydn)**	**1878**	**Talyllyn Railway**	**Built Hughes**
4	**(Edward Thomas)**	**1921**	**Talyllyn Railway**	**Built Kerr Stuart**

No.	Name	Date	Present Location & Owner	Notes
Miscellaneous 0–4–0T and 0–6–0T Locomotives				
5	Jane *alias* Shannon	1857	GWS, Didcot; NRM	Bought by GW 1947 for preservation
12	(Isebrook)	1926	Quainton Railway Society	Geared locomotive
813	(ex Port Talbot Railway)	1901	Severn Valley; GW/R 813 Preservation Fund	
921	(ex Powlesland & Mason)	1906	Leicester Corporation Museum	Sold by WR in 1968
1338	(ex Cardiff Railway)	1898	Somerset Railway Museum, 1338 PF	
1340	Trojan	1897	GWS, Didcot	ex Alexandra Dock Co
1378	Margaret	1878	Pembrokeshire County Museum	Sold by GWR in 1923
2180	Tiny	1868	Dart Valley; NRM	Broad gauge vertical boiler

Builders: 5 – Geo. England; 12 – Sentinel; 813 – Hudswell Clark; 921 – Brush; 1338 – Kitson; 1340 – Avonside; 1378 – Fox Walker; 2180 – Sara)

Note: ex-Burry Port & Gwendraeth Valley Avonside 0–6–0T *Pontyberem* at Didcot was never in the possession of the GWR.
The BP&GV sold it before absorption into the bigger company.

Carriages are the next item for review and here the order is based on successive design families following one another in almost exact chronological order. To get some idea what has *not* been preserved, because of the huge number of variants that existed, readers are referred to Michael Harris' *Great Western Coaches* 1900–1954 (David & Charles, 1972).

Table 3 PRESERVED GREAT WESTERN CARRIAGES

Date	Design	Type	No.	Location
(a) Carriage stock other than diesel railcars and auto-trailers				
1845	4-wheel	1st and 2nd class composite body	—	Dart Valley Railway
1881	Clerestory	Special Saloon	9044	Dowty
1886	6-wheel	Non-corridor Tri-composite	820	Gwili Railway
1891	4-wheel	Non-corridor Brake Third	416	GWS
1891	4-wheel	Non-corridor Brake Third (Taff Vale)	3846	Gwili Railway
1894	6-wheel	Family Saloon	2511	GWS
1894	Clerestory	Directors Saloon	249	Dart Valley Railway
1895	4-wheel	Non-corridor Tri-composite (Cambrian)	238	GWS
1896	Clerestory	Engineer's Saloon	9035	Dart Valley Railway
1898	4 wheel	Full Brake	933	GWS
1898	Narrow Gauge	Saloon Corris Railway	17	Talyllyn Railway
1901	Royal Clerestory	Dynamometer Car	7	Dart Valley Railway
1901	Clerestory	Non-corridor Third	1357	GWS
1901	Clerestory	Non-corridor Third	1941	GWS
1903	Clerestory	Dining Car (body only)	—	GWS
1904	4-wheel	Non-corridor Third	975	GWS
1905	Dreadnought	Corridor Third (70ft)	3299	GWS
1907	Toplight	Corridor Brake Composite	7538	GWS
1910	Toplight	Corridor Third	2426	SVR
1910	Toplight	Corridor Third	2434	Cornish SLPS
1912	ex Taff Vale Railway	Non-corridor Third	1775	private, Bath
1912	Toplight	Nondescript Saloon	9055	SVR
1915	Toplight	Corridor Third	3930	SVR
1916	Toplight	Medical Officer's Saloon	1159	GWS
1921	Toplight	4-wheel Full Brake	1399	SVR

Date	Design	Type	No.	Location
1921	Toplight	Non-corridor Brake Third (low roof)	3755	GWS
1921	Toplight	Non-corridor Brake Third (low roof)	3756	GWS
1922	Toplight	Full Brake	1145	SVR
1923	Toplight	Nondescript Saloon	9369	SVR
1924	Bow-end	Corridor Composite	7976	GWS
1924	Bow-end	Third Diner Saloon (ex Articulated)	9653	NRM
1924	Bow-end	Third Diner Saloon (ex Articulated)	9653	NRM
1925	Bow-end	Corridor Third	4553	GWS
1928	Bow-end	Corridor Third	5085	GWS
1928	Bow-end	Corridor Composite	6045	SVR
1929	Bow-end	Nondescript Saloon	9103	SVR
1930	Bow-end	Special Saloon	9004	Carnforth
1930	Bow-end	Special Saloon	9005	GWS
1930	Bow-end	Full Brake	1184	GWS
1933	Bow-end	Corridor Brake Third	5787	GWS
1932	Bow-end	Composite Diner, end kitchen	9605	NRM
1932	Bow-end	Third Dining Saloon	9627	SVR
1932	Bow-end	First Diner, end kitchen	9615	SVR
1932	Ocean Saloon	King George	9111	Dart Valley Railway Association
1932	Ocean Saloon	Queen Mary	9112	GWS
1932	Ocean Saloon	Prince of Wales	9113	GWS
1932	Ocean Saloon	Duchess of York	9116	DVR
1932	Ocean Saloon	Princess Elizabeth	9118	GWS
1935	Centenary	First Diner, end kitchen	9655	Dowty
1934	Economy	Corridor Brake Third	5883	SVR
1934	Economy	Corridor Brake Composite	6912	SVR
1934	Economy	Corridor Brake Composite	6913	SVR
1934	Economy	Buffet (full length bar)	9631	SVR

Date	Design	Type	No.	Location
1935	Economy	Corridor Third	5952	GWS
1937	Economy	Excursion Third	1285	DVR
1937	Economy	Excursion Third	1295	
1938	Yellow-disc	Corridor Third	1086	SVR
1938	Yellow-disc	Corridor Third	1087	SVR
1938	Yellow-disc	Corridor Third	1111	GWS
1938	Yellow-disc	Corridor Third	1116	SVR
1938	Yellow-disc	Corridor Third	1146	GWS
1938	Yellow-disc	Full Brake	64	Quainton
1938	Yellow-disc	Non-corridor brake third	5539	Llangollen
1938	Yellow-disc	Corridor Composite	7284	SVR
1938	Yellow-disc	Corridor Brake Composite	?	Steamtown, Bellows Falls, USA
1938	Yellow-disc	Excursion Third	1289	GWS
1938	Narrow Gauge	Third	4143	Rheidol
1938	Narrow Gauge	Third	4144	Rheidol
1938	Narrow Gauge	Third	4145	Rheidol
1938	Narrow Gauge	Third	4146	Rheidol
1938	Narrow Gauge	Third	4147	Rheidol
1938	Narrow Gauge	Third	4148	Rheidol
1938	Narrow Gauge	Third	4994	Rheidol
1938	Narrow Gauge	Brake Third	4995	Rheidol
1938	Narrow Gauge	Brake Third	4996	Rheidol
1938	Narrow Gauge	Third, open-sided	4149	Rheidol
1938	Narrow Gauge	Third, open-sided	4150	Rheidol
1938	Narrow Gauge	Third, open-sided	4151	Rheidol
1938	Narrow Gauge	Third, open-sided	4997	Rheidol
1938	Narrow Gauge	Third, open-sided	4998	Rheidol
1938	Narrow Gauge	Third, open-sided	4999	Rheidol

Date	Design	Type	No.	Location
1938	Narrow Gauge	Third, open-sided	5000	Rheidol
1938	Narrow Gauge	4-wheel Brake Van	137	Rheidol
1938	Narrow Gauge	4-wheel Brake Van	138	Welsh Highland
1940	Yellow-disc	Corridor Third	536	GWS
1940	Yellow-disc	Corridor Composite	7313	GWS
1940	Yellow-disc	Special Saloon	9001	GWS
1940	Yellow-disc	Special Saloon	9002	Tyseley
1940	Yellow-disc	Post Office Sorting Van	814	GWS
1941	Yellow-disc	Corridor Brake Composite	7362	GWS
1941	Yellow-disc	Corridor Brake Composite	7371	GWS
1941	Yellow-disc	Corridor Composite	7285	GWS
1948	Yellow-disc	Full Brake	98	SVR
1948	Yellow-disc	Engineer's Saloon	80969	SVR
1948	Yellow-disc	Engineer's Saloon	80972	Tyseley
1948	Yellow-disc	Engineer's Saloon	80974	North Yorkshire Moors Railway
1948	All-steel	Corridor Brake Composite	7372	GWS
1948	All-steel	Corridor Brake Composite	7377	DVR
1948	All-steel	Corridor Third	829	SVR
1949	All-steel	Corridor Third	2119	SVR
1950	All-steel	Corridor Brake Third	2202	GWS
1951	All-steel	First Sleeper	9082	SVR
1951	All-steel	Corridor Brake Third	9083	GWS
1951	All-steel	First Sleeper	9084	SVR
1951	All-steel	First Sleeper	9085	SVR

(b)*Auto-trailers and diesel railcars*

Date		Type	No.	Location
1907		Auto-trailer (70ft)	38	Midland Railway Butterley
1912		Auto-trailer (70ft)	92	GWS

Date	Design	Type	No.	Location
1920		Auto-trailer (70ft)	167	Dean Forest
1932		Auto-trailer (70ft)	190	GWS
1934		Diesel railcar with buffet	4	NRM
1936		Auto-trailer (ex Steam Rail Motor 93)	212	GWS
1940		Diesel railcar, trailer-hauling	22	GWS
1951		Auto-trailer	225	DVR
1951		Auto-trailer	228	DVR
1951		Auto-trailer	231	GWS
1951		Auto-trailer	232	DVR
1951		Auto-trailer	238	DVR
1954		Auto-trailer	240	DVR

Key: GWS – Great Western Society, Didcot
 DVR – Dart Valley Railway
 SVR – Severn Valley Railway
 NRM – National Railway Museum

Table 4 summarises what has been achieved in the preservation of freight stock. As might be expected, it falls short of what has been done in the other rolling stock fields and, of course, far shorter in proportion to the much larger totals of freight vehicles that existed.

Table 4 SUMMARY OF PRESERVED GWR FREIGHT STOCK

No.	Type	Locations
(a) *Vans*		
19	Covered Goods Vans	Dart Valley/Severn Valley/Tyseley/ Bulmers/Didcot/Worcs. Loco. Soc./ National Rly. Museum/9642 Maesteg/ Lakeside
16	Fruit Vans	Dart Valley/Severn Valley/N. Norfolk/ N. Yorks. Moors/Caerphilly/Didcot/ Tyseley/Dean Forest/W. Somerset
3	Banana Vans	Dart Valley/Severn Valley/Didcot
1	Tea Van	Didcot
1	Gunpowder Van	W. Somerset
1	Ventilated Van	Cornish Steam P.S.
6	Motor Car Vans	
	ASMO	Didcot
	DAMO B	Dart Valley
	MOGO	Severn Valley/National Rly. Museum/ Bristol Ind. Museum
	PYTHON	Didcot
4	Insulated Vans	
	MICA B	Dart Valley/Severn Valley/Dean Forest/ Didcot
1	Prize Cattle Van	Didcot
2	Milk Vans	
	SIPHON G	Severn Valley/Didcot/Llangollen
2	Fish Vans	
	BLOATER	Didcot/Severn Valley
1	Grain Van	
	GRAINO	Didcot
5	Narrow Gauge Vans	Festiniog/Welshpool/Vale of Rheidol
(b) *Open Wagons*		
17	Standard Open Wagons	Dart Valley/Severn Valley/Tyseley Didcot/Dean Forest/Bristol Suburban/ N. Yorks. Moors/N. Norfolk/ Middleton
2	China Clay Wagons	Dart Valley/Severn Valley
1	Tube Wagon	
	TUBE C	Llangollen
15	Narrow Gauge Wagons	Welshpool/Rheidol/Brockham

No.	Type	Locations
(c) *Special Wagons*		
1	Glass Wagon	
	CORAL A	Dowty, Ashchurch
1	6-wheel Milk Tank	Quainton
1	Demountable Milk Tank	
	ROTANK	Didcot
3	Bogie bolster	
	MACAW B	Severn Valley/Scottish R.P.S.
1	Well Wagon	
	HYDRA D	Didcot
1	Well Wagon	
	CROCODILE F	Didcot
1	Machinery Wagon	
	LORIOT	Severn Valley

No.	Type	Locations
(d) *Service Wagons, Vans and Cranes*		
26	Goods Brake Vans	
	TOAD	Dart Valley/Severn Valley/Tyseley/Didcot/National Rly. Museum/Caerphilly/9642 Maesteg/Swansea Ind. Museum/Bulmers/Dean Forest/Fawley Hill/Quainton/Chasewater/Llangollen/Steamtown/Mid-Hants/Bluebell/Bristol Suburban/Bristol Ind. Museum.
5	Shunters Trucks	Dart Valley/Severn Valley/Didcot/National Rly. Museum/Fawley Hill
11	Tool Vans	Dart Valley/Severn Valley/Didcot/Dean Forest/Conwy Valley/Bluebell
10	Riding/Mess Vans	Dart Valley/Severn Valley/Tyseley/Didcot
6	Hand Cranes	Dart Valley/Nat. Museum of Wales/Caerphilly/Tyseley/Dowty/Didcot
5	Steam Cranes	Dart Valley/Severn Valley/Dean Forest/Llangollen
2	Ballast Wagons	Severn Valley/Caerphilly
2	Sleeper Wagons	Severn Valley/Didcot
2	Rail Wagons	
	GANE A	Severn Valley
1	Loco Coal Wagon	Didcot

In statistical terms, then, this great achievement of railway preservation amounts to the rather amazing figures which follow. They are hard enough to believe even after they have happened; but what would have been said to anyone who had dared to forecast such numbers 15 years ago when Jon Barlow wrote that first letter to *The Railway Magazine*?

1. Number of locations 67
2. Route mileage of GW Railway preserved 121
3. Locomotives preserved: 107
   (a) Modern passenger classes 25
   (b) Other standard tender engines 11
   (c) Standard tank engines 54
   (d) Miscellaneous 10
   (e) Narrow gauge 7
4. Carriages preserved 104
   (a) Corridor 32
   (b) Open 21
   (c) Non-Corridor 16
   (d) Passenger Vans, Mail Vans 8
   (e) Saloons 17
   (f) Refreshment Vehicles 10
5. Freight stock preserved 202
   (a) Traffic Vehicles 132
   (b) Service Vehicles 70
6. Numbers of stations and depots preserved 33

In addition, of course, there is so much GWR preservation which does not lend itself to any reasonable sort of list. In an earlier chapter we saw that many Great Western things are still around for the satisfactory reason that the organisation which compulsorily purchased the old company still finds them useful in their original role. Much else has also survived without any conscious effort at preservation because a new use is found for whatever it may be. A prime example is Brunel's beautiful train shed at Bristol, used as a car park. Another is a length of the old Wye Valley line south of Wells in Powys which has been converted to the B4567 single track road. Because of the way in which the railway was built with overbridges and underbridges, connections are made with other roads in motorway fashion. At the same time the curves and grades, severe by railway standards are far superior to those of the A470 trunk road on the other side of the river. It is a real fun drive.

Even so, apart from the occasional footpath or nature trail, in general little has been done to make use of the majority of those sad miles of GWR roadbed whose tracks failed to survive the Beeching period. Although many disused bridges and viaducts enhance the landscape, one cannot say the same of many of the derelict stations. A favourite use for those which have been disposed of is some useful but hardly beautiful purpose such as the premises of a scrap car dealer. Other stations have been luckier in that they have been converted into nice country houses such as Avonwick Station on the old Kingsbridge Branch. The occupier even advertises holiday accommodation for railway enthusiasts in the GW Society's magazine *Great Western Echo*, and other railway journals.

There are several disused ex-GWR canals, aside from those which have remained in use or which have been restored. Unlike old railways, the fact that canals have uses over and above their transport role for such things as drainage and water supply, usually keeps some kind of maintenance in being, even if navigational aids such as locks and tow-paths fall in or otherwise become unusable. One might note the Monmouthshire Canal (from Newport to Crumlin and to Pontymoile), various waterways in the Taunton Area – one particularly likes the name of the Grand Western Canal which led from Taunton a short distance to Tiverton – and the Liskeard & Looe and Par Canals in Cornwall.

Absolutely unamenable to statistical assessment is the private and personal approach to preservation. One particularly nice thing about preserving GWR things is that anyone can do it; just one ticket with the sacred words printed thereon adds its own fallen leaf to the vast landscape. For obvious reasons the GWR rarely made or ordered anything which did not have the name or initials prominently displayed upon it and there can be very few household articles indeed from table knives to chamber pots that the old company did not own. Remember that in addition to being train, ship, horse and cart, lorry, aeroplane (for a short time) and bus operators, the GWR also owned docks, hotels, hostels, houses, stables, garages, refreshment rooms, canteens, bakeries etc, on a large scale.

The firm was also a big-time publisher; even leaving out of account ephemeral things like posters, timetables, extra trains notices and the like, a reasonable collection of GWR literature would fill a good-sized bookcase. The amount is such that a good-sized book is needed to chronicle its full extent; in fact, Roger Wilson's excellent *Go Great Western* (David & Charles 1969) needs 200 pages to do just that.

This leaves quite out of account books *about* the GWR published by others, of which the numbers are enormous. The *Great Western Railway Magazine* was primarily for the staff, but it was so good that many members of the public subscribed also. The proceedings of the Great Western Railway Lecture & Debating Society, containing papers by many great railwaymen, are another source of nostalgic wonder at spacious days and ways now gone for ever. E. T. Macdermot's monumental three-part two-volume *History of the Great Western Railway* was the worthy summit of the company's publishing effort. All these things find their place in the list of items to be preserved. Pride of place in the writer's own modest collection goes to a letter confirming an offer of employment as a 'Junior Surveyor & Draughtsman' at £275 per year, but easily next comes a set of those magical 'Boys of All Ages' books, mainly by W. G. Chapman, describing various aspects of building and running a real railway. The way in which they never 'talked down' to their (quite often) youthful readers is an example to the present-day world of railway publishing. Over 150,000 copies of books were sold over the years from 1923 to 1939, and many will still be preserved. Deeply regretted is the disappearance of a number of the enchanting jig-saw puzzles made for the GWR by the Chad Valley Company, just another example of the surprising scope of the possibilities, although occasionally they come up at auctions of railwayana where they fetch high prices.

While GWR foodstuffs can hardly have survived, their containers might. The *Great Western Echo* recently expressed regret that bottles of Great Western Special Scotch Whisky could no longer be found. It is still possible, however, to buy Great Western Champagne, but this really excellent beverage (now called sparkling wine although it is in fact the real thing) actually has nothing to do with our line but instead comes from the celebrated Great Western vineyards 100 miles west of Melbourne, Australia.

Coming down from the sublime to something in which your author took a greater interest in pre-war days, one notes boxes of Great Western Assortment biscuits provided by Huntley & Palmers of Reading for the dining cars, complete with a GWR express train running round the tin.

One cannot even begin to assess the amount of small preservation which has been done privately except to say that the quantity is enormous. Furthermore, all the big preservation enterprises cherish their small things almost as much as they do their Castles and Manors. Platform seats and trolleys, station signs, slot machines, enamelled advertisements, milk churns and even (in the case of two Severn Valley members) a Karrier mechanical horse and trailer are examples of what is displayed and (often) used.

Lastly, since human involvement is what preservation is all about, we must salute those who not only restore things but also themselves, as GWR relics. This is done by having made, with all the expense of bespoke tailoring, one's own suit of one of those distinctive Great Western uniforms. And, of course, putting on a set of those deservedly celebrated Great Western manners to go with the clothes. For was not the way GWR staff dealt with their often tiresome public a good deal of the reason behind the immense liking for things Great Western that has made everything described in this book possible?

Appendix

Paper submitted by the author in 1969 to the Chief Planning Officer BRB for exploitation of 'Steam entertainment'

1968 TRANSPORT ACT
DIVERSIFICATION
Exploitation of Steam Locomotive Entertainment Value

1. **INTRODUCTION**

    It is a fact that the spectacle of a steam locomotive at work has a considerable appeal to a large and growing section of the public which has demonstrated willingness to pay for its pleasure. This is evidence of a business opportunity taking into account the continued existence of suitable steam locomotives and servicing facilities in private and other hands. (Table I) Exploitation of 'steam locomotive mania', however, is contrary to Board policy; the question arises whether this should be modified.

    Perhaps the point should be made that the appeal of the steam locomotive as a static museum exhibit is very limited; this has been clearly demonstrated by the poor financial results achieved by the various railway museums.

    On the other hand enterprises that provide 'live steam' as an attraction have gone on from strength to strength.

2. **MARKET**

    In considering the market, distinction must be made between the railway enthusiast who is prepared to spend a good deal of time and money on his hobby but who exists in limited numbers, and others with only a casual interest in railways or no real interest at all: but who are prepared to spend a certain amount of time and money on a visit or outing. These latter customers exist in very large numbers indeed. With this in mind it is suggested the following facilities should be offered:—

    (a)   Steam train trips – for the casually interested
                   (see section 2.1 below and Table II)
        estimated contribution to net revenue – £110,000

    (b)   Steam exhibitions – for the casually interested
                   (see section 2.2 below and Table III)
        estimated contribution to net revenue – £50,000

    (c)   Steam rail-tours – for the enthusiast
                   (see section 2.3 below and Table IV)
        estimated contribution to net revenue – £90,000

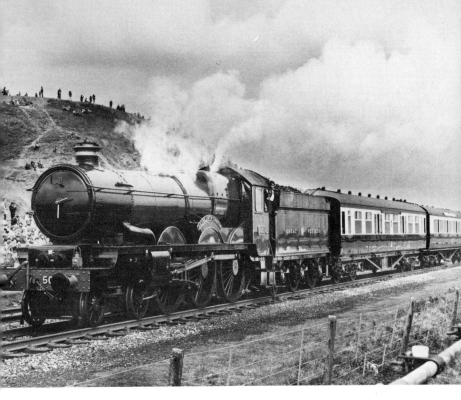

Above: The Rainhill display of 25 May 1980 marking the 150th anniversary of the Liverpool & Manchester Railway. No 5051 *Drysllwyn Castle* plus two restored GWR coaches from the Severn Valley Railway take part in the parade. *John Titlow, courtesy GW Society*

Below: One of the failures: *St Stephen* hauling a parcels train and seen here in early BR service. Alas none of this class has been preserved. *Author's collection*

Above: No 5051 *Drysl_lwyn Castle* with the GW Society's Sunset Limited between Stratford-on-Avon and Hatton on 19 January 1980. *David M. Scudamore*

Below: Encouraging the new generation: schools day at Didcot, July 1978. *Courtesy GW Society*

There is some additional revenue to be obtained by collaboration with the various loco-owning bodies in the use of steam locomotives for filming and publicity purposes.

As with other obsolete forms of transport, now that it has become of no practical value, the steam locomotive's attraction as a spectacle is increasing, so growth beyond these figures is certainly possible.

2.1 Short Steam Train Rides

The intention would be to capture the large 'casual interest' market with rail-trips over quite short distances. Preserved steam engines would be used of which many suitable exist (Table I). In general the route chosen would be short, reasonably convenient for a base at which steam locomotives are available, with little or no traffic on the days in question, but with prospects of attracting recreational custom. Operation on a regular basis, on, say, twenty Sundays every year would be suitable.

As an example of a line which meets all these requirements, one might cite Birmingham (Moor Street) to Stratford-on-Avon, where there is no regular train service on Sundays, six trips might be run in the course of a day. In this case traffic would arise at both ends and it is suggested, therefore, that results would be rather better than the more typical operation costed in Table II(b). With a possible target of six operations across the country, including some lesser ones, contribution to net revenue exceeding £110,000 could be expected.

(Birmingham–Stratford, York–Scarborough, Carnforth/Barrow and Didcot–Reading were the lines suggested.)

The way the market for this type of operation has grown is set out in Appendix II(a). About $1\frac{1}{2}$ million steam trip journeys are expected this year on the eight principal steam tourist railways, representing traffic receipts of some £250,000, but it must be borne in mind that their profitability is limited by the fact that they have to provide track, buildings and coaching stock exclusively for this tourist operation. In fact several (but not all) depend on volunteer labour to a greater or lesser extent and one, the B.R. Vale of Rheidol line makes a small loss. This is in clear contra-distinction to the co-operative effort proposed in which use is made of idle track, carriages, buildings, etc., provided for normal transport purposes at other times.

It might be mentioned that a number of those who own or control the steam locomotives have also gained experience on the successful steam tourist railways, so that the profit-sharing arrangements proposed (Table II(b)) are intended to provide a fair basis for the use of the commercial know-how which has been gained in this rather specialised field.

161

2.2 Steam Displays

These would take the form of 'Open Days' or exhibitions held on suitable sites, at which famous steam locomotives would be on show in steam, together with a display of the latest B.R. equipment and possibly other attractions such as traction engines and portable miniature railways. There would be trade stands, etc., and an opportunity for a B.R. promotional effort, emphasising the new by contrast. Although the appeal will be mainly aimed locally, some of the steam locomotives on show would have brought rail-tours to the exhibition from other parts of the country, the two activities being complementary.

Such open days are of course currently being held on an experimental scale, but a target might be fixed at twenty-five a year with net receipts (see Table III) at £2,000 on each occasion, making £50,000 per annum in all. This represents one or, in a few cases, two shows per Division each year.

2.3 Steam Rail-tours for Railway Enthusiasts

Having regard to membership figures for the clubs concerned, and taking into account past expenditure, it is estimated that there are 10,000–15,000 railway enthusiasts who are prepared to spend a substantial sum, say £10 annually, on steam rail-tours at £4–£6 a time. There is also proven scope for those sponsored by educational authorities for school-children and for some with a non-railway objective to bring in participants with a more casual interest in steam.

The requirement is for a train of open stock with buffet facilities, haulage by a famous main line steam locomotive and a schedule with certain characteristics:—

(i) Starting and finishing point accessible to a centre of population;

(ii) good scenery and an interesting locomotive task;

and, perhaps, (iii) stops for photography and visits of railway interest.

Demand in general coincides, or can be made to coincide, with days and routes on which spare capacity (stock/line/manpower) is available, mainly out-of-season week-ends.

A target attainable in two or three years' time would be to run seventy rail-tours annually, with a choice of approximately the same number of suitable Saturdays and Sundays to have them

162

on. This is well below the numbers run in recent years and adequate patronage can without doubt be achieved. Based on the results of a typical rail-tour (see Table IV), contribution to net revenue is estimated to be £90,000–£100,000.

3.   PRO AND CON FOR STEAM ENTERTAINMENT

The attraction of the proposal lies in an estimated net contribution to revenue of £250,000 with no capital expenditure, together with a useful bonus of publicity and goodwill.

Possible drawbacks lie in five directions, viz: that such an operation would:–

(a)   Impair the image of a forward looking rail system.
(b)   Lead to accidents which would not otherwise have occurred.
(c)   Interfere with the punctual operation of other trains, inducing a net loss of goodwill.
(d)   Involve an administrative effort disproportionate to the results obtained.
(e)   Lead to embarrassment in refusing certain owners for good reasons while others were accepted.

3.1   Image

There seems little doubt that, as it has gradually disappeared from regular use, the steam locomotive has changed its image of dirt and despair for a much more attractive one. This is likely to have been due to the good condition to which the preserved locomotives have generally been restored and favourable treatment from the press.

An image likely to be fostered by a programme of steam excursions is that of enterprise in turning a one-time burden into a benefit; there is also the corollary that, in failing to take advantage of what appears to the public as a clear commercial opportunity, the corporate image is presently suffering.

3.2   Safety

There are clearly dangers in allowing the indiscriminate use of locomotives in unknown condition on rail tracks, and it is suggested that the essential participation by locomotive owners should be confined at the outset to those who have had previous experience in providing steam-power for rail tours on B.R., involving about fifteen locomotives. Others could later be included when their ability to meet stringent technical requirements has been demonstrated, any long runs only being undertaken after an apprenticeship period on short trips.

It is true that experience so far has shown that danger is not

163

likely to arise provided that reasonable precautions are taken, of which the following may be mentioned:—

    (i) A supervisor in the locomotive cab for all steam movements.

    (ii) Independent boiler examination and insurance.

    (iii) Strict mechanical inspection as for any other rail vehicle.

Provision of footplate staff and supervisors who retain their skill in handling steam power would only present problems, even then not insuperable, should a protracted interval in steam operation occur.

3.3 Interference With Other Traffic

This matter is connected with safety in that a locomotive kept in good mechanical condition and properly handled is not likely to delay other traffic through break-down. Late running through other causes has been common on rail-tours, and while not serious in itself, there have certainly been cases where other traffic has been interfered with. Where this has happened, however, the rail-tour in question has usually included complex movements, frequent changes of locomotive, and/or running on lines with insufficient spare capacity.

A solution can be found by insisting on simplicity and continuing to prohibit certain lines to steam traction, also by careful scheduling to include adequate arrangements for coaling and watering the locomotives, which, in the absence of B.R. facilities, will be the responsibility of the locomotive owners.

Just as in the matter of safety, only those owners who can demonstrate their abilities in this direction also should be allowed participation, if satisfactory results are to be attained.

The shorter trips proposed (section 2.1 above) are, of course, unobjectionable on this particular score.

3.4 Administrative Effort

Again in this matter, requests for complex arrangements have sometimes led to an excess of administrative effort on the operating side, barely counter-balanced by the fact that, on the commercial side, all publicity and booking has been handled by the railway society sponsoring the tour. This latter arrangement would continue.

To reduce the planning effort it would be possible, without detriment, once a repertoire has been built up, to discourage tours other than those for which operating instructions can merely be re-issued with slight amendments. The shorter trips would only be a matter of initial arrangements then repetition; as regards longer ones, simplicity is desirable as discussed for other reasons with consequent reduction of administrative effort.

3.5 **Problems of Refusal**

Some embarrassment has been caused in the past by certain locomotive owners whose persistence was not equalled by their abilities and sense of responsibility. The problem here is to say "No" in such a way that it is taken as final.

A possible solution would be to have a limited list. This would actually be an extension of the present arrangement whereby one locomotive (No. 4472, Flying Scotsman) is allowed to operate, but without the rather unsatisfactory features that a monopoly tends to have; quite apart from limiting the market through repetition, that is. The list would be of people and organisations rather than locomotives and would be selected on the grounds of experience, technical ability and sense of responsibility of those in charge as well as the resources available in the way of locomotives and maintenance facilities. Any entry on the list would be reviewed periodically and it would be a clear feature of the arrangement that this review was not merely a formal one.

In this way the smaller owning bodies would be encouraged to come to an arrangement with one of the better organised ones which had earned a position on the running list, and would not deal direct with British Rail.

J. B. Hollingsworth
Senior Planner
April 1969

TABLE I

SUMMARY OF PRESERVED LOCOMOTIVES

	Category I LARGE	Category II MEDIUM (Suitable for shorter trips only)
A. Available and in the hands of people who have previously provided steam power for rail-tours.	10	6

B. Other locomotives available.	16	29
C. Possibly available if enough incentive.	28	50
D. Unlikely to become available.	4	10
Totals	58	95
Forecast of eventual availability A+B+50% of C	40	60

Note: If forecast levels of traffic are achieved, allowing for a proportion of rail-tours requiring more than one locomotive, each will be needed on an average of four times per year. This is reasonably in line with the capacity and resources of most of the owners, representing as it does an annual mileage of 800 or so.

Service and stabling facilities, in the main rented from B.R.B. or others, exist at the following places:—

Ashchurch	Doncaster	Longmoor
Ashford	Hereford	Peterborough
Carnforth	Keighley	Philadelphia
Didcot	(Haworth)	(Co. Durham)
Dinting	Leeds	Tyseley
		York

Only those locomotives are included which have at some time been in possession of British Railways since 1947. Small and/or ancient ones have been omitted, though some of these would form excellent attractions if steamed on 'open days'.

TABLE II

MARKET FOR STEAM TRAIN TRIPS AND THE BASIS FOR THE FORECAST

A. Growth of General Interest

In order to show how interest has been growing in a general way, the figures are given for the aggregate passenger journeys

166

on five tourist railways with live steam; Tal-y-llyn, Ffestiniog, Ravenglass & Eskdale, Romney Hythe & Dymchurch and Vale of Rheidol. All were well established at the beginning of the period and are representative.

Year	Passenger Journey
1960	530,000
1962	550,000
1964	600,000
1966	710,000
1968	1,020,000

There are a further three operations of significance, Bluebell, Worth Valley, Dart Valley, the last two being of very recent birth. It is expected that, when the traffic on these is taken into consideration, passenger traffic on these eight lines will, in 1969, exceed $1\frac{1}{2}$ million and £250,000 in value, and, moreover, without the total market being satisfied geographically.

B. **Short Steam Trips on B.R.**

The results that might be expected from typical short steam trips on B.R. are given below. It should be noted specially that the costing is intended to show contribution to net revenue on the assumption that otherwise idle assets are used. Marginal costing is justifiable here because if the equipment is *not* idle, the trains should *not* be operated.

The loco-owner's fee is based on £1 per mile loaded plus £50 insurance.

Length of trip each way	20 miles
Occasions per annum	20
Stock	2 trains
	each 2 BSO, 4 SO
Seats	320 each train
Fare	£1 return
Number of trips	6
Total number of passengers	1500
Average number per trip	250
Gross receipts	£1500
Trains crews, carriage servicing, special opening of signal and booking offices, etc.	£200
Loco-owner's fee and expenses, including insurance.	£340
Net receipts	£960

Allow sponsoring
    society's profit.   £230
    (50% above £500)
                                                     ─────
                                                     £730
Car park fees, rail fares
    to reach starting point,
    platform tickets, etc.   £250
                                                     ─────
        Contribution to net revenue
            per occasion   £980
                                                     ─────

        Contribution to net revenue for a
        typical steam-ride operation per
        annum is £19,600.

TABLE III

RESULTS TO BE EXPECTED FROM
A TYPICAL 'OPEN DAY'

		£
Gate money 12,000 at 5s. 0d.		3,000
Steam train rides 2,000 at 2s. 6d.		250
		─────
		3,250
	Expenses	1,000
		─────
	Profit	2,250
Allow share of profit to		
organising railway society		625
(50% above £1,000)		
		─────
		1,625
Car park fees, rail fares to reach		
show, profit on sale of		
refreshments, etc.		400
		─────
Contribution to net revenue		£2,025

Note: The expenses are based on those for Birmingham
    (Tyseley) 'open days' in September 1968 and May 1969,
    while the 'gate money' has been estimated on a lower basis
    on the grounds that a typical 'open day' will not be quite
    so successful. Others may justify more elaborate and
    expensive arrangements, e.g. the recent 'open day' at
    Cricklewood.

TABLE IV

MARKET FOR STEAM RAIL-TOURS
AND THE BASIS FOR THE FORECAST

A. **Growth of Railway Enthusiasm**
Taking the period from the beginning of modernisation until recently, the following details are relevant:—

	Number of steam locos in use on BR	*Number of railway enthusiast clubs*	*Members*
1955	17,955	8	2,500
1968	4	19	14,300

In addition, a large number of locomotive and railway preservation societies has come into existence and, although the total number of members is not known, over forty further societies are members of the Association of Railway Preservation Societies, only a handful of which were in existence in 1955.

B. **Growth of Steam Rail-tours for Enthusiasts**
In the five last years of steam traction, B.R. attempted to cater for the demand during 1964–1966 and the following rail-tours were listed as running, hauled both by service and by preserved steam locomotives:—

1964	70 tours
1965	90 tours
1966	104 tours

In 1967 a policy decision was made (later reversed) not to cater for this traffic, which reduced the number run that year to 78. This decision was then taken again after the end of steam in 1968, except for one locomotive No. 4472 'Flying Scotsman' which continued to run under contract.

Sampling carried out during this period indicated that typically the loading was as given below. There were a few cases of cancellation compensated for by some private tours which were run in addition, as well as others so popular they needed repeating. Fares varied from 30s. 0d. to £16 (The B.R. 'last steam train' at 15 guineas was not the most expensive).

The section of the market which took its steam rides on ordinary service steam trains cannot be estimated but again sampling on suitable services in the last years indicated it to be quite large.

169

C. **Results to be Expected from a Typical Rail-tour**

Two examples are costed:–

	(i)	(ii)
Stock	(2 BSO (Buffet (7 SO	(2 BSO (Buffet (6 SO
Seats	512	448
Seats sold	450	400
Fare	£5	£4
Receipts	£2250	£1600
Train crew, carriage servicing	£200	£150 (see note 2)

Loco-owner's fee
    insurance and
    expenses
	£600
	(second loco
	in use
		£300
		(one loco)

Net receipts	£1450	£1150

Allow sponsoring
    society's profit
    (50% above £1000)
	£225	£75
		(see note 1)

	£1225	£1075
Ancillary fares	£100	£75
Buffet Car profit	£75	£50
Contribution to net revenue	£1400	£1200

Contribution to net revenue
per tour £1300

Notes: 1. The sponsoring society would have an opportunity to supplement profits by selling railway literature, etc., en route.
2. The costing is intended to show contribution to net revenue on the assumption that otherwise idle assets are used. Marginal costing is justifiable here because if the equipment is *not* idle, the train should *not* be operated.

July 1969
CPL.5/3/2

Index